Endorseme

"I think I needed to read this story. I don't have children on the spectrum so I don't think I would have thought I *needed* to read it. But let me be clear. I *needed* to read this book. It reached me in such a fundamental way. I think that is why I cried so much while reading it. Tamara's revelations on coveting basically punched me in the face. I didn't realize I had been so upset lately because of my covetous reactions to those close to me. I feel as if I have been purged of those negative emotions. I am so happy that this book fell into my inbox when it did!"

– Lisa Russo Leigh,
Precision Editing Group

"Through Tamara's eyes, I saw normal doesn't exist for any culture, society, community, or even family. But each of us can accept what is normal for our self, and thrive. It feels good to be normal again."

– Jeffrey Probst,
an abnormal author

"As a 'next level' parent, I can't think of anyone more qualified than Tamara to support you on your journey. Tamara is the ultimate cheerleader, and her message is hopeful, compassionate, and most of all real. *Normal For Me* is like a warm hug—reassuring, reaffirming and courage-inducing."

– Jenna Evans Welch,
New York Times Best Selling Author

"As a parent of an adult son with autism, I was touched by Tamara's book, *Normal for Me.* Tamara writes of the struggle of raising two sons with autism, while trying to balance her busy life as a wife, mother, and active member of her community. She includes excerpts from her journals, and her husband, Justin, adds insight into what he was going through at the time. Throughout the book, Tamara shares how her faith in God helped carry her through her darkest days, and helped her grow spiritually, while going through the ups and downs of raising sons with autism. She shares what she learned along the way, and offers steps parents can take to make this journey easier. I believe this book can offer encouragement to parents of children with special needs and help them navigate through the "new normal" for their lives."

– Doris Dill,
Author and Mother of a child with autism

"This book will resonate with more people than those who face disability challenges in their family. Tamara shares that we are not alone on this planet. There are others fighting the same or equally challenging things in their lives. I especially enjoyed Tamara's real candor, insight, encouragement, prayers throughout the book, and the fact that she got mad! I needed to read that. I particularly related to the night she prayed for angels. I also enjoyed Justin's supportive perspective from a father's point of view. This book is *NORMAL FOR ME!*"

– Debbie Ihler Rasmussen,
Author and Mother of children with ADD & ADHD

"Whether you are raising a disabled child or know someone who is, *Normal for Me* will help you understand the needs and realities of parents raising special needs children. It gives an honest and hopeful story of normal people responding to extraordinary challenges. It is worth reading."

– Kirsten Johnston,
author of *Letters from a Christmas Elf*

"Tamara's raw vulnerability and honesty pull you into her life story while giving you the tools to cope with your own trials and problems. This book can help every person who has struggled with broken dreams and harsh realities. I felt renewed hope and energy after reading *Normal for Me*."

– Lisa Johnson,
Educator

"So many times we look at the lives of others and wonder, *Why can't my life be like theirs?* But if you could see deeply into the things we all hide behind closed doors I think you would quickly change your mind. Tamara opened those doors and shows us how to take joy where we can, learn from the good and the bad, and move forward. Always move forward."

– Jay Walther,
Podcaster

Endorsement for *Diagnosis Survival Guide*

"This *Diagnosis Survival Guide* is such a needed thing. We have to talk about these things and let others know they are not alone and will be ok."

– Christine, *R.N.*
Cancer Survivor

"I think this *Diagnosis Survival Guide* should be something therapists should give to their patients to get them from fear to hope."

– Lynn Wilkinson,
Occupational Therapist

"When the diagnosis comes, when the news isn't good, when my life script includes something I never wanted, I long for a trusted companion to breathe hope into my sudden fearfulness. In the *Diagnosis Survival Guide*, Tamara Anderson offers a how-to guide born of experience. Life may not be the normal we anticipated but Tamara assures we can live rich and full."

– Peggy Sue Wells,
author of *What to do When You Don't Know What to Say*

"I really like that the *Diagnosis Survival Guide* is a powerful quick read. It offers great advice. Tamara gives the reader a piece of her heart and her struggle, which makes it human. It is well written, easy to read, and therefore should be well received."

– Jeanne Boehmler,
Special Education Teacher

NORMAL *for* ME

LEARNING TO LOVE *and* ACCEPT LIFE'S DETOURS *with* GOD'S HELP

Jaycie- You are normal for you & God loves you! Tamara K Anderson

TAMARA K. ANDERSON

Daily Hope Publishing

Normal For Me: Learning to Love and Accept Life's Detours with God's Help

All the scriptural verses shared in this book are from the King James Version of the Bible.

Book cover and interior design by Francine Eden Platt
Eden Graphics, Inc. • www.edengraphics.net
eBook design by Dayna Linton
Day Agency · www.dayagency.com
Cover photo by Scott Betts

Library of Congress Control Number: Pending

978-1-7321469-0-7 Paperback
978-1-7321469-1-4 eBook

Published in the United States by
Daily Hope Publishing

Manufactured in the United States of America
10 9 8 7 6 5 4 3 2 1

With love to Justin, my parenting partner and best friend.
Thank you for adding and contributing your comments throughout this book.
Your name should probably also be on the front cover.

TABLE OF CONTENTS

Dear Friend,

Thank you for taking this journey with me. This truly has been a labor of love to write. There were many times when my editor would ask me to dive in and share more details. I recall one evening telling my husband, "I honestly don't remember."

Have you ever had that happen with something painful and awful? That is called repression. My brain literally repressed the memories—buried them deep and threw away the key. I was in survival mode at the time, and years later, I could not recall how I made it through—only that I did. So, I had to pull up what little journaling I had done and read about those years. What I read made me remember—and weep. Yeah. There is a reason I had forgotten how awfully hard it was . . . and there was a reason I still didn't want to remember. It was hell. It was like trying to remember the battle scenes of my life. I didn't want to remember. But I did.

I remembered and wrote this in the hope that some person out there battling through life and struggling to survive day by day will know *they are not alone*. They will know that someone else has waged a similar war before and survived. I wrote my heart into these pages with one thought, *that it would give someone hope—hope that they too can survive*, that they too can make it one more day, and then the next. That they too can lean on God in the darkest times of their lives and that He can help them get through it. That is the only way I made it through—sometimes one minute at a time, one day at a time, and then on to what eventually became a month and then a year. And then someday, like I did, hopefully they too will look back and think, "How did I survive that soul-wrenching experience?" And they won't remember. No, like me they won't remember the details, but they will remember that it was awful, and it was hard.

I must confess that remembering has filled me with gratitude to God for getting me through.

So, let's get to the story that I have tried so hard to forget, because it is a story worth sharing after all. I wish I could paint myself as a hero, but I am going to write what really happened, and sometimes I was weak and felt angry, exhausted, and numb. So, forgive me for being imperfect. I was and am a work in progress.

– Tamara

NORMAL FOR ME

Have you ever had a regular day that morphed into a terrible, soul-wrenching day capped off with a life-changing moment?

My "Normal For Me" Story

For me, it all began on a beautiful spring day in Arkansas, following a long, cold winter. After dinner, I glanced out the window and saw couples and families walking down the street enjoying the warmth and sunlight as it faded into evening. The end of a gorgeous day beckoned.

My husband, Justin, and I decided to follow suit and take the children on a walk. Getting the kids ready to go anywhere was a bit like herding grasshoppers.

Jordan was the leader of the pack at age seven and the only one of my four children who could verbally communicate with us at the time. We asked him to get his shoes . . . and if he didn't get distracted, he might just come back with them without too many prompts.

Nathan, age six, was our "stealth bomber." Quiet and sneaky, he preferred streaking through the house with as little clothing as possible. So, going anywhere with him usually required some redressing. (Parenting tip: don't put Nathan's shoes on until you walk out the door, or he will take them off, and you will do it all over again.)

We called Jacob, age two and half, our escape artist. He climbed anything he shouldn't climb and got into everything! In the perspective of an old fable, Nathan would be our tortoise, and Jacob would be our hare—so wickedly fast, it's a chore to catch him!

Still at the carry stage, Noelle, our baby girl was easy. No chasing required. Just plop her into one half of the double stroller, buckle her up, and she was good to go. Jacob got the seat of honor in the other side of the stroller, so we didn't have to run after him every five seconds.

Thirty minutes *after* deciding to take a walk, we exited the front door to breathe in the beautiful spring evening.

Our calm, successful excursion lasted less than five minutes. Halfway down the street Nathan began a huge tantrum. He did the "leg drop" kids do when you're holding their hand, forcing you to either drag them or carry them. Screaming at the top of his lungs, he brought chaos to the quiet evening. No words . . . just crying. He didn't want to go on a walk and nothing we could do or say could convince him otherwise. We even tried bribery, but it is hard when your words aren't understood.

My husband scooped Nathan up and took him home, and I dutifully finished the walk with the other three children. As the sun commenced its descent, my heart sank with it. By the time I returned home, I felt overwhelmed and flooded with despair.

Once I had the children settled for the night, I fell on my knees, my heart aching. Questions spilled from my anguished, weeping soul: *Why do we have two children with autism? Wasn't one enough? Why is life so hard? Why can't we just go on walks like a normal family? Why can't we be a "normal" family?*

Somewhere amidst all my blubbering came a firm, yet kind answer. God simply whispered, "Tamara, this *is* normal for you."

This simple truth surprised me as it resounded over and over within me.

The more I thought about it, I realized I had never known "normal" as other families experience it. I have two "typically-developing" children, and two little boys blessed, and challenged, with autism. That is my normal—what God gave me to love and cherish.

Once I saw myself in that light, asking all those "Why" questions I'd been so intensely anguished over became ludicrous. I had fallen into the unhappy trap of comparing my family, my children, and my life to others. I needed to free myself from those comparisons and embrace the gifts with which I'd been blessed. *Tamara,* this is *your life!* These are *the challenges you have been given.*

God pushed back my fog of despair and doubt and lifted me to a higher level of understanding. No, my life wasn't what we would call "normal." But, then again, whose life is "normal?"

> **JUSTIN:** I remember that day for many reasons. First, it was totally normal for us to try and do regular things most families do, only to have them blow up on us. I felt discouraged. I still remember carrying Nathan back home that afternoon with him on one shoulder crying and screaming while trying to carry a tricycle in the other hand.
>
> The second reason I recall this experience is it flipped a nerve in Tamara and sent her into a personal pity party. This is something we both did at times, and still do occasionally.
>
> Third, Tamara received clear inspiration that changed both of our worlds forever. I cannot emphasize enough how key this epiphany has been for us both.

World-Wide Norms?

There are different norms for cultures all over the world today. In India, it is a compliment to burp after a meal, whereas it is not very polite in the United States. I have a good friend who lived in China for a few years, and she said the people go grocery shopping every day, so their food is fresh. Since she didn't want to go shopping every day, she would load her cart up very high and full, and she was gawked and stared at by the Chinese people because not only did she have blonde hair, but she also had a very full shopping cart.

In England, they drive very fast in very small cars

on the left-hand side of the road. It is normal for them. It's a shock if you are from America and used to wide roads with big cars where we drive on the right-hand side of the road. That is normal for Americans!

There are differences all over the world. I am sure if we could visit the many villages in Africa alone, we would find many unique ways to dress, speak, eat, dance and behave culturally.

There are also differing religious norms out there!

Love and kindness are universal. Life-changes are universal. Nothing will ever play out perfectly normal for anyone's life. There will be bumps in the road and detours for all of us.

I guess my point is, there is no universal, across the board "normal" if you are a resident of this world. What is normal in one place, is not in the next. What is normal for one person is not for the next.

Physical Differing "Norms"

We *all* have circumstances that make us feel abnormal or different. We *all* have unique challenges to face. Each of our lives are different from each other and is uniquely "normal for us." It is what crazily makes us who we are!

Some challenges we face are apparent because they are physical in nature. With these kinds of disabilities, people often wish to help. My sons appear "normal" physically upon first glance, so people often turn away from us or judge us when they react out of the norm. For example, when we visit a crowded place, my sons are often oblivious to the fact that there is a natural boundary around other people, and you shouldn't intrude on someone's personal space. So, I will often have to pull them back if they are standing too close to someone in a line.

Other times, Nathan will skip by people in a crowd and accidentally bump someone. He is now 6'1" and is a big boy, but he acts like a giant two-year-old. People don't know he has autism when he bumps into them. They just see a big teenager who has plowed into them. *Sigh!* People often react aggressively in voicing their displeasure: "Hey buddy! What are you doing?" I *hate* disclosing my life's story to complete strangers, but in these cases I usually have to stop, apologize, and explain quickly, "I'm sorry sir (or ma'am.) He has autism and doesn't understand he has bothered you." We get all sorts of reactions after that. Some people immediately calm down. Others just keep spouting angrily, "Well, keep him under control, would you?" *Yes*, I think. *I am doing my best.* Then I run off to catch my giant toddler.

Events like this are embarrassing, and there are times I must weigh how much emotional energy I have before I take Nathan out in public. He is a bit of a wild card, and we never can accurately predict how he will react to different scenarios. Sometimes he *loves* the places we take him. But other times he will throw a tantrum in the lobby of a hotel and scream at the top of his lungs, "NO DISNEYLAND!" What kid says that? Oh! That would be my child. But I am not going to stay holed up in my house forever because I would go insane. So, we keep venturing out with our now very big boy.

I will tell you that we did get him an iPad a few years ago, and it has been a godsend. If Nathan is getting agitated, we can often save our excursion if we pull out his iPad or hand him our phone to play on. Yes, you might think it is the "easy way out." Please don't condemn me until you have walked a mile in my shoes. You see, he is too big for me to physically control anymore. I can't just pick him up and take him outside like I would a two-year-old. He outweighs me by about a hundred pounds. So, I will do my best to calm my child, and then I will hand him his device so the rest of the family can enjoy the activity. It's only fair to us (and to you).

I don't want to give the impression there are no bright spots in our autism battle. I have met some of the most wonderful people because of my two boys with autism. I have been the recipient of prayers, kindness, love, and service. There are many angels out there (both seen and unseen), and God knows just when to send them to help.

I recall attending Noelle's sixth grade play. I arrived early because I didn't know how Nathan was going to react to this "change in the schedule" and my husband was out-of-town, so I knew I was going to do this solo. Nathan was mad from the moment we arrived and threw a tantrum in the parking lot.

I eventually coaxed Nathan inside and got him seated by handing him his iPad. Unfortunately, I didn't have the Wi-Fi password for the school and Nathan was upset again and kept yelling, "Wi-Fi!" Since the performance hadn't started yet, I left Nathan with Jacob and went off to find a teacher and beg for a Wi-Fi password. The teacher I found didn't know what the password was for guests but said she would try to find out. I went back to sit by Nathan, still agitated, while our other son Jacob (who has high-functioning autism) sat as far from us as he physically could on the same row. He was totally embarrassed to be seen with us because we were causing a scene by this point.

Dear God, where are you? We could use some help!

Bless that sweet teacher! She came running back to me and put her password into Nathan's iPad. He immediately calmed down and enjoyed his device while I sat back and was eventually able to calm my "fight or flight" symptoms enough to enjoy Noelle's performance.

To this day, I am thankful for that dear teacher I didn't even know. She saved that night for me! She was my angel and an answer to my desperate prayer. My only other option at that point would have been to take Nathan out and miss the performance entirely. I would have been devastated because Noelle had worked so hard to memorize her lines and had been practicing for months. I wanted to see her perform and she deserved to have her mother there to see her success.

My friends, can you see how important it is to not judge people too harshly? Each person's "norm" is different from another's. We are often doing our best with the crazy circumstances life seems to throw at us. It is important to attempt to see beneath the surface a little before judging someone. Kindness goes a long way. I invite you to be kind and to be an answer to someone's desperate prayer. You cannot know someone else's inner struggles unless you have walked a mile or two in their shoes.

JUSTIN: Jacob is so embarrassed when Nathan blows up in a public area. Jacob's autism makes him less socially mature than boys his age, though this great kid has made amazing progress. But having Nathan throw a tantrum or stand out because of his behavior is hard for him, and it stresses him out. Tamara and I have learned that even though this causes stress, we just roll with it. Any other reaction would only make life tougher.

Let me take you to a basketball game where Nathan, a 6' 1", 250 pound "man," starts screaming, "Go home!" over and over. I have learned to just laugh at it, or I will physically start bleeding anxiety. You can then imagine others thinking he means the losing team should "go home," and that causes me to laugh some more. So, we try to help calm Nathan down so those sitting near us can enjoy themselves while they wonder what type of parents we are.

I used to feel so terrible when he exploded, and then some person would turn around a look at me like I'm a bad dad, and it made it worse. It becomes a cycle of self-doubt, frustration, anger, and pity. Learning to separate myself from the situation was the first step to healing, but it takes time.

Inner Differing "Norms"

Some challenges we have are deeply personal and known only within the confines of our soul. They include insecurities, doubt, anxiety, depression, and mental illness. I believe inner struggles are the most challenging because they are invisible to other people. No one walks around with a sign that says, "Depressed," "Insecure," "Lonely," or "Heartbroken *again*."

I have felt many of these inner struggles at different points in my life. I remember in college feeling broken after a long relationship ended. Looking back, I am sure I dropped into a situational depression with my heart crushed. I vividly remember waking up and wishing the break-up had all been a dream. But each time I awoke, the pain was still there. I couldn't wish it away. I got up, went to class, did my homework, and repeated it the next day. My soul ached. I prayed and prayed and prayed my heart out to God, dumping all the raw emotions on Him. I was blessed with a few close friends that seemed to carry me and listen to me as I processed my change in situation.

One night, several months later, I was praying once again and felt like I needed to go somewhere peaceful. I went to one of our local churches decorated for the holidays. There were crowds of visitors all laughing and enjoying the holiday season.

I ran into some old friends, including my old flame. He looked happy. Suddenly, almost like magic, my date (God) took my burden—that raw pain I had been carrying around for many months—from my shoulders. I felt free. I felt alive. I felt whole. I felt awed and grateful at the miracle God had wrought in me. Christmas meant a little more to me that year because I looked at the babe of Bethlehem as my personal Savior a little differently than I ever had before. "Surely He ha[s] borne [my] griefs, and carried [my] sorrows . . . and with His stripes [I am] healed."[1]

To those of us who have battled with these inner struggles, may I tell you that you are not alone, even though you may feel lonely. God is there for you daily wherever you are, just as He was there for me. I have learned this in my moments of greatest heartache. I have come to know God truly does love me and care about *me*. He is literally my Heavenly Father, and like any good Father, He desires to help His children.

JUSTIN: When Tamara says God is our Heavenly Father, I want every person who believes in God to think about this for a second. No, don't just think about it, meditate on this, reflect, ponder, pray... whatever you do to connect with God. You need to know this fact if you want to survive and thrive in this life. A majority of religions from Christianity to Hinduism to Judaism call God our "Father." To me, this means God is approachable, loving, caring, listens well, and knows how to help me individually.

My place of peace varies, but a good heart-felt prayer is always a safe bet for me. I feel a natural connection with God when I pray. My favorite part of prayer is to stop and listen, or see how I feel, and I often get impressions or ideas that help me along.

1 Isaiah 53:4-5

I have learned it is important to find people you trust to help with your inner struggles. Perhaps it will be a parent, a spouse, a friend or a counselor. But I have learned it isn't good to keep everything bundled up inside us all the time. Burdens are easier when shared with "angels" God sends along the way.

I am thankful for my "Normal for Me" experience on my knees that spring evening many years ago—it raised my sights to a different level. It was a reality check that helped me realize, "Yes! You *are* different. That is the way you are. Get over it! Get on with your life and quit complaining about it!" We each have physical and mental or emotional differences. Let's be kind to one another and cling to God as we trudge through obstacles.

THE CALM BEFORE THE STORM

HAVE YOU EVER WISHED a weather predictor for life existed? Wouldn't it be great if we could turn on our own personal TV every morning and receive a weather forecast just for us? "Tamara, your weather forecast for today is a foggy morning that will burn off to bright sunny skies the rest of the day." Or, "Major tornado heading into your life tonight. Prepare yourself and hunker down!" Wouldn't it be great to know a life-changing hurricane was heading for you a week, six months, or a year before it hit?

In the late fall of 2000, my husband found out his company needed to transfer us from Southern California to Bentonville, Arkansas. Moving clear across the country, far away from family, frightened me. But as we prayed, we felt it was the right decision for our little family. So, in February 2001, my husband and I found ourselves on the way to the airport en route to find a new home in Arkansas.

We never made it to the airport. Along the busy California freeway, my husband and I were involved in what should have been a fatal car accident. I still look back and shudder as I remember how unexpectedly it happened, and how quickly my life could have been over. I learned in an instant how fragile life is, and how much each moment is to be treasured. I can't explain why we survived, only that perhaps God knew we still had things to learn and accomplish. I am so glad we did not leave our two little boys orphans that day!

> **JUSTIN:** The accident was a humility moment for me. Though I was not "at fault" for the accident, I learned that day it was time to stop driving like a NASCAR driver and start taking more responsibility for those around me when I drive. One step towards maturity!

Thankfully, Justin was treated in the hospital as an outpatient with a few stitches. I, conversely, spent the next week and a half in the hospital. Even though I had been wearing a seatbelt, I still ended up with a broken collarbone, broken ribs, punctured lung, and blood pooling around my internal organs (just a few of many injuries). To make a long story short, I was in bad shape. I am a walking testimony of the healing power of God and proof of the power of prayers.

Because we were incapacitated, my parents took

Jordan, and Justin's parents took Nathan for the next month so we could heal and recover.

If you knew in advance, what would you do to ready yourself for the emotional barrage of moving to a new place beyond the quick support of family and friends, or enduring a painful car accident followed by a lengthy recovery? Both of these situations were minor storm bursts in my life when compared to the hurricane diagnosis of autism which would soon follow, but they also presented us with learning opportunities on the road of life.

Unfortunately, the Early Life Storm Warning System has not been invented yet (maybe someday). The next best thing is the lessons we learn from passing through the storm. We can even benefit if we will pay attention to other people's storm experiences and apply those lessons in our lives. Just as watching a natural disaster on television might prompt you to buy extra supplies, create a family emergency plan, or purchase extra insurance, being wise enough to learn from our own and others' hindsight can prepare us for the next storm cycle. And there's always another storm.

Thankfully, the storms are always followed sooner or later by sunshine and rainbows. And then another storm. It's a natural law, and you can't be angry at it, anymore than you can complain about the law of gravity. You just put your storm preparation in place so you are better prepared for the wild wind, floods, and lightning.

Reflecting on my life before the autism diagnosis, I wish I could go back and give myself three little bits of storm prep advice:

1. Be grateful and enjoy the calm moments whenever they come, no matter what your circumstances. You never know when a life-size hurricane is looming.
2. Learn the cycle of service in life. I'll explain this later in the chapter, but it is an important life lesson I needed to learn.
3. Make a plan and keep moving forward. Lack of planning leads to inaction, and that keeps you from making progress and improving any situation you are experiencing.

Be Grateful and Enjoy the Calm Moments

When Nathan was born, I felt a great calm. I remember counting his fingers and toes and proclaiming him perfect. He was so sweet—straight from heaven.

He and Jordan were only sixteen months apart, and I had to play referee to keep the baby safe from a busy toddler intent on touching baby's eyes, ears, nose, mouth, etc. Thank goodness Nathan has always been a sturdy size and survived being "loved" by his big brother.

As he grew, Nathan had a speech delay. I vividly remember going to his eighteen-month checkup concerned about his lack of progress. Our pediatrician told me, "He is fine. Some kids don't talk until they are three."

Though consoled a little bit, my mama intuition tingled. Maybe my weather radar was sending me alarms—indicating a storm forming off in the ocean. But life was busy and good. Truthfully, there were times that the daily stresses got in the way of simply enjoying the moment. But every moment spent in appreciation gave me spiritual strength that fortified me for the storms to come.

Since no clouds were visible, it was easy to push away any uneasy feeling and simply bask in the joyful moments. I'm so glad I did. While it is a fact that "into every life a little rain must fall" and while it's only common sense to be prepared for an occasional shower—or even hurricane—it is a mistake to spend too much time worrying about storms that haven't happened yet. That only casts shadows on your present happiness. Looking at some of my journal entries from that sunshine period, I can still rejoice in the small but wonderful gifts that filled my heart and our family with happiness. Here are some quotes from my journal entries in 2001:

- Justin taught Nathan to slurp milk from a spoon and we all laughed. The next time Nathan started laughing before he slurped, and the milk flew all over. We all laughed so hard our tummies hurt. Ah—what a sweet family we have!
- Jordan and Nathan played and wrestled together tonight. I love my boys and my husband!
- Nathan's birthday! I have enjoyed holding Nathan in my arms and singing to him as I put him down for his nap. He sang, "I am a Child of God" almost word for word with me, and I was so amazed! He is such a sweet little boy.
- Nathan learned to give kisses tonight! He is so cute, and he even said, "Love you!" He is finally speaking more and that is comforting.

- *Jordan got home this afternoon with many hugs and kisses and what a whirlwind of activity he is! Both he and Nathan are so happy to be home. They ran around and chased each other and played. Justin and I are so happy to have our little family back together.*

Finding those little daily moments of joy were an important part of enjoying the calm before the storm. In the hustle and bustle of daily life, it is sometimes easy to miss the moments of grace showered upon us. But every moment we spend in gratitude is a profound reminder in the dark times that the sun always rises. Practicing gratitude in the calm times gives us strength and courage in stormy times.

While I was busy enjoying gratitude (and unknowingly preparing myself for the storms ahead), life had a few more lessons for me. The next in line was the role that service would play in my journey.

The Cycle of Service

Due to the accident, I instantly went from a person who served my family and others, to one who could not care for my family or myself. I had two little boys in diapers, and I couldn't use my right arm. I don't know if you have ever tried to change the diaper of a wiggly little boy one-handed, but it is nearly impossible!

I couldn't bathe on my own, dress on my own, nor cook on my own. I felt worthless! I found it surprising I could be twenty-seven-years-old and feel like a ninety-year-old woman! I remember the first week home from the hospital, getting up, getting ready (with my husband's help), and then being so tired I had to go back to bed. Yep, I was pathetic!

JUSTIN: Talk about pathetic! We couldn't do much, and when I say "we" I mean "Tamara." It was very hard for me to see her go from a strong, active, vibrant person to someone who struggled to do the basics. The first few weeks we tried to master simple personal care: cleaning up, moving around the home, preparing basic meals. I quickly learned that our home had functioned so well because Tamara was so capable.

This was an eye-opener for me in many ways. I was learning that running our home had become very complex. Our high-energy children multiplied the complexity and yet Tamara had been able to provide love and care to all of us. She was also very active in our local church, serving the community with a variety of activities and individual ministering.

I couldn't replace her. Not in the slightest. I was humbled, and learning this was very important to me for years to come. So, at this time I knew we needed help.

This is when a dear friend, boss, and mentor at my work surprised us with some help: free home cleaning for a few months!

This was a small revelation to me. I didn't marry Tamara to have her always cleaning. Sure, I did "my part" which I confess, at times seemed like a lot. It left me deeply grateful for how Tamara blessed our family. But I felt inspired that if we could afford some help cleaning our house from

> time to time, we should keep doing this long after the accident and recovery. Since then, we have been blessed to hire some help occasionally. We still have daily and weekly chores for me and the kids. I don't want them to grow up not knowing how to work!

We needed help during the accident recovery! In addition to the house-cleaning, people brought us meals, helped clean and prepare our home to go on the market, and watched our little ones. Kindness after kindness continued to our family from the wonderful members of our church and community.

I don't know how we ever would have made it without them! I still tear up as I think about those wonderful people *I learned to love because they served me.* Isn't it funny how that works? I didn't know gratitude turned into love. This lesson of swallowing my pride and allowing my family to accept service was such a crucial lesson for me to learn pre-diagnosis. I never knew you could learn to love by being served.

This was the beginning of my continuing education on learning to love. And it definitely is continuing education—because this is a university course we will take our entire lives. I learned the cycle of service is a cycle of love. Not only does serving others help me learn to love them, but allowing others to serve me teaches me to love as well.

This was an important lesson for me to learn during the "calm before the storm," because in the ensuing years I would need more help. God blessed us with many angels along the way.

Before the accident, I had this false notion I needed

to be strong enough to do everything myself—that it was a sign of weakness if I asked for help (from anyone except God). But how else was God supposed to answer my prayers for physical help, if not through someone here on earth?

I still struggled sometimes asking for help—even during the accident recovery. I didn't want to call people to help me when my husband was traveling and I physically couldn't put the boys down by myself, but I had to swallow my pride and do it. I knew that my collarbone would never heal if I kept using it.

I knew God wanted to teach me to love more purely, so that I could better emulate the pure love of Christ and be filled with charity toward others. I had only ever given the service—not received the service. And so I was thankful to learn even more over the ensuing months that love can grow on the receiving side of charity.

> **JUSTIN:** I believe in angels. We are God's hands on this earth and good people from our church were ministering angels for our family.

The cycle of service strengthens us both when we serve others and when we allow them to serve us. It strengthens us by allowing us to experience true unity. Our hearts fill with charity as we serve others — we see them as God sees them. And then when we are served, our hearts are also filled to overflowing by the realization that we are so deeply loved and cared for, by God and family and friends —some we didn't even know we had. Those bonds of love that connect us to others provide strength and comfort that we continue to draw on through the storm and beyond.

An example of this charity is the love we developed for Justin's Aunt Marilyn, who came to stay with us the week the boys came back to us after spending a month with grandparents. Justin and I were still recovering from the trauma our bodies experienced due to the accident, and we couldn't keep up with two very busy boys.

Tamara's Journal, March 14, 2001

Marilyn has been such a dear and I wish she didn't have to leave. The kids love her too. She is such a charitable person—always thinking of others before herself. I admire her tremendously.

It was amazing how much our family grew to love aunt Marilyn in one short week. Her service to us will forever be embedded in my heart. She was truly a mentor to me as I learned the blessings of both serving and being served. My gratitude turned quickly to love.

What a blessing it was to learn to love those people who served me as I was recovering from the accident. These were little miracles which blessed my life in the calm before the storm. And oh, how I was going to rely on the full cup in the days ahead.

Make a Plan and Keep Moving Forward

Tamara's Journal, March 6, 2001 (Just after the car accident)

Tonight, we had a long talk with Justin's mother Judy, a Special Ed teacher for twenty-plus years and well trained in helping kids with special needs. She felt impressed to talk to us about Nathan. On and off, we have had concerns about his development. In caring for him (as I recovered from the accident) Judy saw his struggle with his language and communication, and his lack of eye contact. She felt he needed to be assessed and told us the steps to take. I felt like a prayer of mine had been answered and my concerns for Nathan weren't just me being an obsessive mother. So, tomorrow, Justin and I will sign a consent form to have Nathan's development assessed.

Even though I know it is the right step to take, the conversation overwhelmed me.

Can you see the storm clouds forming on the horizon? We didn't know what type of storm we were in for, so we kept trudging forward—blissfully unaware of how much our lives would be changed over the ensuing years. But looking back, this was definitely a clear warning that my normal was going to be anything but.

Soon it was time for our sons to come home. It was then that Justin got a full dose of storm warning as well.

JUSTIN: I remember picking Nathan up at a truck stop, halfway from our home and my parents. You can imagine my excitement to see Nathan. When he got out of their car, he and I looked at each other for a moment and . . . nothing . . . no recognition, happiness, or anything. I remember my heart dropping into my gut right then because I knew something wasn't right. I shook it off quickly and showered him with my love and affection.

When any type of storm or disaster seems imminent, government agencies always encourage the people in harm's way to "make a plan." We didn't understand the magnitude of the storm that would hit us soon, but we did our best to make a plan on how we could help Nathan. With the new move, we had to get Nathan assessed and get him services in Arkansas.

I filled out paperwork for Nathan to get help with his speech and other developmental delays. Even though I was nervous about going, I felt a sense of relief to take some action. It made me feel like I wasn't helpless.

Nathan started speech therapy and on the first day he said several words: down, ball, bead, bubble, cup and pop. I had a moment of hope that this was a small worry that would soon be in our past. That hope didn't last for more than a few weeks.

Tamara's Journal, September 7, 2001

My soul has been heavy today because the speech therapist said the occupational therapist (OT) recommended Nathan for a psychological evaluation to check for autism. In my heart, I had ruled that out—he's too social, right?

Can you see how dark the storm clouds are brewing in the weather of my life? The storm had drawn closer. I just didn't want to look up and see all the signs, because I knew if I did it would mean an end to my "normal" path in life. Couldn't I stay in this sunshine-filled world for a few more moments?

By March 2002, we made the decision to start Nathan full-time at the Benton County Sunshine School. As I talked to the teacher and went into his classroom, I felt a weight just lift off me. I had been torn about having Nathan go to school for such a long amount of time since he was only three-years-old. I had a strong conviction that it was important for a child to be at home, but Nathan needed a little extra help.

This was a real dilemma for me. I wasn't working outside the home so I could raise my children and teach them. Jordan was only doing pre-school a few days a week and now Nathan (who was younger than he was) was going to go daily!

I think God helped me reach a point with Nathan where I knew he needed help I couldn't give him. It was hard to get over that hump, because parents are supposed to teach their children. Parents are supposed to help them learn to speak and do things for themselves.

But sometimes you have a child who needs more specialized help. I didn't get a degree in speech therapy, and so I didn't know much about helping children with challenges learn to speak. This was part of the plan where we needed to move forward—even though it was hard.

When we are buffeted by our own storms, it can seem overwhelming. But inaction never is the answer. We can move through our storms and back into the sunshine one step at a time. Sometimes it's a step of faith and courage, because we can't see in front of us. But without acting, we stay in the storm much longer than necessary, when clear skies and smooth sailing might be just around the corner.

One of the other principles of storm preparation is to create a personal network of people you can call on to help you when you need aid. I didn't realize it at the time, but God was helping us expand this network of people to help us with Nathan.

I am glad I figured out he needed help. It was a relief to have others share the burden—because it was heavy to try to carry it on my own. As you can see from my entries below, I was still wavering between blissful denial and acceptance that our lives were going to take an unplanned detour.

Tamara's Journal Entries, May 2002 — Jan. 2003

- Nathan is understanding more. He said "stop" yesterday when he got frustrated at preschool. He has started therapy too, so hopefully, this will help. Now if we say, "Nathan, come here" he will mostly come, which shows he is understanding more. I am grateful to the Lord for blessing him.
- Nathan continues to make more progress in speaking and understanding which lessens tantrums. I am grateful he understands when I say, "we are going bye-bye," "get in your chair," or "time to go night-night." Tonight, he said, "want candy," and "more cracker."
- We do worry about Nathan. He seems to have digressed since he got out of school for the

summer. I guess it goes to show how much it was helping him and how he does need it.

- (A week after Jacob was born) Poor Nathan had a hard time tonight. He has had so much change happen in the past week, and he cried and threw a tantrum tonight until I calmed him by holding him. Then he cried when I left the room and it was time for him to go to sleep. (I think he misses being the baby and getting "mama" time.) I stayed with him for a while and then I had to go nurse the baby, so I left the door open so he wouldn't cry. He came downstairs and sat on my lap as I nursed the baby.

  As he sat there on my lap he said, "Nathan cry." This is the first time I have heard him refer to himself as "Nathan." Poor little guy! My mom took the baby and I rocked Nathan to sleep. This is going to take some adjusting for all of us.

- Nathan is learning and using words to communicate what he wants now a little more and we are grateful for all the progress he is making. Sometimes I do wonder if he will live anything of a "normal" life. I hope so, but there is something wrong—I just don't know what it is. I guess deep down I still hope he will "grow out of it," but I don't know. Part of me wants him to be diagnosed while the other part of me still clings to hope and faith.

  I guess sometimes it is hard to gain an eternal perspective of "life." One thing I do know is the Lord knows and understands our family and our situation, and I draw comfort knowing everything is going to be "okay." I just don't know what "okay" means.

I read a little of a book on Autism today and some descriptions fit Nathan to a "T" and others don't. I am not sure what to think.

- It was a hard day! My frustration with Nathan hit its pinnacle today. I wish he could communicate, and I could explain to him why he can't play the computer all the time. Anyway, Justin sat down and talked to me and I cried and cried because Nathan isn't going to be "normal." I know it, but I don't want to believe it.

These last few journal entries show that in my mind I had moved from, "everything is going to be fine" to wondering if it will be. There truly was a battle raging inside my heart and mind. I could no longer deny the storm was upon us.

One part of my mind was clinging to hope that we would find the "thing" which would help Nathan. I wanted this to happen with all my heart! I was fighting for this to be true for a long time.

The other part of me knew something was wrong. Call it motherly intuition or a gut feeling. I knew Nathan was different. I knew something was wrong. I knew it didn't normally take kids this long to learn to talk. I just wanted it to be something curable—something we could "fix."

I think one of the hardest things about a life detour is part of you wants to live in the "happy" land of naivety, but there is another part of you that wants desperately to know what is wrong so you can solve the problem. Those two sides of you are at war with each other. When you find yourself in this situation, tremendous courage is needed to move forward and finally discover the truth. Truly, God opened doors for us, and we had to have the courage to walk through them.

JUSTIN: I had forgotten so much of this until I read these journal entries. We had no clue and we probably didn't want to have a clue about this if it meant Nathan would be formally diagnosed. Denial is the enemy of progress.

We all experience the "ostrich effect" where putting our head in the sand seems better than tackling bad news. I won't say Tamara and I fought against the diagnosis. That isn't true. We were uneducated, unsure, and enduring as best we could.

We teetered between showing the courage of moving forward and quietly sliding backward scared of where that would go. I'm so glad Tamara and I shuffled our feet a little more toward the courage side of this experience. It was time to get our heads out of the sand.

Although I didn't consciously set out to make a plan, looking back, I can see that we were being guided to resources, people, and information that would eventually form part of a "battle plan" as our family moved forward on a new path.

Sometimes we don't plan because it seems overwhelming. But I've discovered over time that simple plans can be as effective as complex plans. A plan can be as simple as a single goal, a single step you can control as you deal with your storm. Once you have a plan, it is much easier to take a step, and then another. And the great thing about that is taking even a small action empowers you, moves you from being and feeling helpless to being someone that can walk through the storms, full of confidence and good cheer.

Taking action reminds you that God has not left you alone and helpless. And as you make a plan and tackle your own storm, you will also quickly learn there's truth in the old adage, God helps those who help themselves. That doesn't mean we don't rely on faith and humility and prayer, on charity and service, and all the other spiritual gifts God graces us with. But we demonstrate faith by our actions, and as we act, we open ourselves up to miracles in our lives.

I am thankful I could enjoy little daily moments of joy during the calm. I also was grateful to have learned important lessons about the cycle of service and love. Lastly, I am glad that through planning I could continue forward progress in preparation for the ensuing storm. I was blessed to begin developing a personal network of people to help us along the way—including specialists. The "calm before the storm" was now officially over and the storm was upon us.

DIAGNOSIS — DEAD END OR DETOUR?

As a teenager, I used to dream about what my future would entail. I imagined graduating from high school, going to college, serving a mission for my church, getting married, graduating from college, and having a beautiful family that would be quite perfect.

I dreamed my children earned superb grades (because I did), excelled as athletes (because my husband did), sang in choir, loved going to church, graduated with honors, volunteered for missions, married, and founded beautiful families of their own.

Of course, life rarely unfolds as we dream or plan.

Expectations

I remember attending a class at church one evening many years ago, where a good friend of mine spoke about "expectations." She explained many of the bumps in life happen from "unfulfilled expectations" and we need to learn to communicate our expectations in marriage and in life.

We also need to hold realistic views of expectations. Take my dream of the ideal life. In my dream life, everything was roses and ticker-tape parades with a cherry on top. There was nothing worse than a skinned knee that could be kissed away or a misunderstanding that could easily fixed. There was no room for the things that come to everyone, sooner or later: sickness, loss, heartache, and (like the old joke goes) taxes and death.

This concept of "unfulfilled expectations" was an eye-opener to me. The more I thought about it, the more I realized the truth in her advice! I always seem to have an idea in my mind about how I think a certain situation should unfold, and if it doesn't turn out how I imagined it would, I choose to be upset or frustrated.

I now understand better that while it's wonderful to have expectations, and strive for them, they must be balanced with a healthy dose of realism. This is different than being negative. Let me give you an example. I heard the story of a former POW from Vietnam who spoke about his experiences and that of his comrades. He explained that prisoners who died the soonest tended to be the overly optimistic ones. They had unrealistic expectations of rescue and when that didn't happen, they tended to quickly lose hope and stamina. In contrast, those who held firmly to hope of rescue or escape, but also tempered that with the realities of their situation, tended to have higher survival rates.

Hopefully we will not experience such a traumatic event, but no matter what curveballs life throws at us, learning to combine optimism with a calm acceptance that we can't dictate every detail in life can help us face the unexpected with balance.

I realized I would often feel that way about things which changed in life! I figured out I needed to try to *pause* when life threw me an unexpected twist and think about how I was going to react—because often I could not control the situation, but I could control how I reacted to it.

Sometimes our unfulfilled expectations are life-changing: having a child with autism, being diagnosed with cancer or another debilitating illness, experiencing the unexpected death of a loved-one, or infidelity. What do we do then? Who do we talk to about that? How do we come to grips with these life-altering events?

I think I have figured out two secrets which keep me going. They are things I had to learn the hard way by walking through my own unexpected detour through the wilderness with God.

1. God has a *much* better plan for my life than I do.
2. He is the one I need to talk to when life's expectations get inexplicably altered.

So, when your expectations are changed, talk to God. When life puts you on an unexpected detour, talk to God. When life shatters, talk to God.

The questions for me then became: Do I have faith God will guide me in the way He knows is best? Do I believe the challenges I encounter are things I can overcome with God's help? Do I believe He will help me?

Those questions may be easy to answer in the good times. But in the hard times, when expectations have been shattered . . . well, that is when true faith is tried and either made stronger or falters. I had to live through major detours to learn a little bit more about myself, God, and expectations.

Back to my story: I did graduate from high school and college, learning and growing along the way. Much to my blessing, I served a mission for my church and married a wonderful and fun young man, Justin Anderson, with whom I can say I am equally yoked.

Having children hasn't been as easy as I thought it would be (and I am sure every parent can echo those words). But the challenges I faced with an autism diagnosis turned my world upside down.

Where is the Promised Land?

There is this great story in the Old Testament which talks about Moses leading the children of Israel out of Egypt. I think it perfectly exemplifies the emotions of hitting a life detour.

The children of Israel had lived in Egypt for over 400 years as slaves to the Egyptians, "The Lord said, I have surely seen the affliction of my people . . . and have heard their cry by reason of their taskmasters; for I know their sorrows." God told Moses, "I am come down to deliver them out of the hand of the Egyptians and bring them up out of that land unto a good land . . . flowing with milk and honey,"[2] even a Promised Land.

Following the plagues, Pharaoh let them leave with Moses. After they fled, Pharaoh pursued them with six-hundred of his finest chariots and blocked their exit on one side, while they were "entangled in the land, the wilderness hath shut them in."[3] With cliffs too tall to scale on their north and west and the Red Sea to their east, they were at a dead end.

When the Israelites saw Pharaoh's army in pursuit, they panicked. They were literally stuck with nowhere to go. They were "sore afraid" and "cried out unto the Lord."[4] They also complained fiercely to Moses, "Because there were no graves in Egypt, hast thou taken us away to die in the wilderness? Wherefore hast thou dealt thus with us, to carry us forth out of Egypt?"[5]

Basically, they were complaining—Did you bring us here to die? "We did tell thee in Egypt saying, Let us alone, that we may serve the Egyptians? For it had been better for us to serve the Egyptians, than that we should die in the wilderness."[6]

This, my friends, is a life detour. The children of Israel were unhappy with their lives as slaves to the Egyptians, but it seemed easier than what they were facing—a dead end with certain death.

There are times in life when we may feel this way—like we have been backed into a corner. Things have

---

2 Exodus 3:7-8

3 Exodus 14:3

4 Exodus 14:10

5 Exodus 14:11

6 Exodus 14:12

gone from bad to worse and now we don't see any way out. We are stuck. We may even be wondering, "Where is the promised land?" I came for the happy ending, not the dead end! Basically, we want to skip from Act 1 of life to Act 3 without the growth that happens in Act 2 because muddling through the wilderness of Act 2 is awful and hard.

What do we do when this happens? Do we weep and wail like the children of Israel? Do we cry and complain to God and those around us we feel have "caused" our predicament?

If you had asked me years ago how I would react if I was faced with a similar situation, I am sure I would have said I would have had faith and would have trusted God and Moses. It is easy to think you will be brave, but my courage completely failed me when Nathan received his diagnosis. I wish I could say differently.

I will never forget the drive home from Little Rock, Arkansas, where Nathan (then four years old) received the diagnosis of autism. I sobbed and wept uncontrollably. I don't think my husband had ever seen me cry so much. Finally, he pulled the car to the side of the road and tried to help calm me down.

I wept because my beautiful—and fragile—dreams for my sweet Nathan were smashed into such tiny shards, they could never be put back together. I physically felt as if my heart, like my dreams, had shattered beyond repair. I cannot adequately describe the anguish and crippling pain I felt. It was devastatingly real! I didn't want the diagnosis to be autism, because there is "no cure."

Some of the pain was for Nathan. He would never experience life as I had. School would be different. He would probably never play sports. He probably would never go to college, serve a mission, get married, or have children of his own.

Some of the pain I felt was for me. Being the parent of a child with a disability was not in my plan. It was not what I had dreamed my life would entail. I didn't want that burden. I didn't want that life. I wanted a normal life. I wanted normal kids. I wanted my dream life.

Basically, I wanted to go back to Egypt. I was just as bad as the Israelites. I was backed into a corner and I was "sore afraid." With hope shattered, I couldn't see a way out and grief assailed me. I was looking for my promised land before I even went through the wilderness.

I also "cried out unto the Lord." I had experienced too many "little miracles" in my life to deny He was there. I knew God lived and was aware of my grief and pain. I knew He could fix it. I just didn't know how.

> **JUSTIN:** I think many fathers have a really hard time with these life detours for this exact reason . . . we have built up our own expectations of being an amazing dad. For me, that meant taking my child fishing, coaching their sports team, or giving them dating advice from a man's perspective.
>
> Dads want to have sons they can wrestle, tickle, rough house, and be crazy with. I wanted to teach Nathan to throw a ball, jump something scary, or other "normal" things.

Like Tamara, my expectations were completely shattered when Nathan was diagnosed. I didn't cry like she did, probably because we needed one parent to keep it together, but I felt hollow inside. The role I was supposed to play for this child was completely ripped away from me. I was feeling such selfish thoughts inside, even while I was providing comfort and encouragement to Tamara.

My prayers to God were more for her at first. I was really worried if she could get through this grief quickly enough to help move things forward for Nathan. This is a very helpless feeling and something no parent wants to feel. But for dads, this can be just as hard because we often lock things up inside.

Could I help Tamara get past this grief? Would I be able to resolve my own? Prayer was going to be a key way to get to these answers quickly.

The Grieving Process

I wish someone had told me I would go through the grieving process for a little boy I could never raise "normally." I wish someone had explained the importance of being gentle with myself. As a believer, I couldn't understand why I was so angry with God or why I felt so depressed when my prayers weren't answered the way I desired. I wish I wouldn't have felt guilt on top of grief for the emotions raging within. Realizing I would experience the grief cycle would have helped me recognize the emotions I was feeling as "normal."

There should be a psychologist or grief counselor on

hand for anyone who faces a life-changing diagnosis. Maybe not everyone needs it, but I did, though at first, I wasn't in any emotional state to talk with a counselor. But after the initial shock, grief counseling would have helped.

Be gentle with yourself. Grieving is a natural step considering the loss of "normal" dreams and expectations.

I didn't know it then, but looking back, I can see my husband and I went through many of the stages of grief as we dealt with Nathan's autism: denial, anger, bargaining, depression, and acceptance.

DENIAL: Oh yes! On the three-and-a-half-hour drive home from the hospital my husband and I decided we wouldn't tell anyone about the diagnosis. How is that for denial? We couldn't even talk about Nathan's diagnosis of autism for a few months. It was too hard. We had to let our hearts heal a little and allow our brains time to wrap themselves around the fact our life would be different than we had planned or expected.

I remember telling the diagnosing physician that one of Nathan's therapists said Nathan couldn't be autistic because he let you touch him (this is a trait of some autistic children, but not all). The diagnosing physician said before we left she would be glad to say she was wrong, if we could prove it. I left her office with this one sliver of a thought in my head. We would prove her wrong! He was not autistic!

Denial? You bet!

We told Nathan's preschool teachers the hospital would send us the report with the diagnosis in several weeks, which was true. Meanwhile, we pretended

Nathan would be fine. Sigh! If you know someone going through the grieving process after a diagnosis, give them time to come to terms with it. It is a bitter pill to swallow for some. Maybe they will want to talk, and maybe they will live in denial for a while like we did. Here's proof I was living in Denial-land:

Tamara's Journal, May 22, 2003

It was a good day but long day! Nathan woke up early and I stayed up too late. I was reading more about autism and I just get frustrated because so many of the traits don't fit Nathan. I feel they didn't eliminate everything pre-diagnosis.

What I didn't understand when Nathan was diagnosed was each child with autism is different. One might be low functioning, have speech delays, and poor eye-contact but be okay with touch. Another child with autism might have so many sensory issues that they can't handle anyone touching them, tags on their clothes irritate them, and they don't communicate well.

I must point out, it is not good to live in "denial" for too long. I have known people who completely want to ignore their child has a disability for years—even after a full diagnostic team has helped make a proper diagnosis. This is not the right way to live. It will not solve the problem at hand, and only causes bigger problems later. Sometimes parents seek diagnosis after diagnosis until they get one they are happy with. I'm not sure it is fair to the child nor the parents in the long run.

The Egyptians are coming whether you deny it

or not. So, it is better to eventually face the fact you have hit a detour. You cannot pretend you are living in Egypt when you are at the edge of the Red Sea.

Our denial stage lasted for several months. But once Nathan's pre-school teachers received the diagnosis, the amount of help he received surprised me.

Since Nathan now had a "label," I feared he would be treated differently in a negative way. What I didn't realize was that being treated differently meant he would get a *lot* more help. Once he had a diagnosis, people knew what techniques had been shown to help children with autism and they used them, leaving me humbled and grateful.

ANGER/BARGAINING: Yes, I was mad at the diagnosing physician. How dare she condemn my child to a lifelong disability? I know this was totally irrational of me, but that is how I felt. I was also angry at myself for having Nathan immunized. One of the theories at the time was immunizations caused autism. I now understand immunizations didn't cause his condition. But at the time, this thought led to a significant self-anger.

It is important not to fall prey to these guilt trips. When you get a tough diagnosis, everyone has an opinion of what caused it. They mean well, and often have valid ideas. But adding guilt to grief isn't the best way to approach diagnosis. We cannot change the past, so internalizing guilt over what you "should have done or shouldn't have done" doesn't change the outcome of the diagnosis. We can only change the future. So quit looking back. Look forward.

I held anger for my husband, too. I think Justin

cruised on through to the acceptance point of the grief cycle while I was still in the anger phase. I was angry at him because to me, this seemed like "giving in" or insufficient faith that God could heal Nathan.

JUSTIN: She was really mad at me for a time. And I did not enjoy this one bit, but she didn't realize that I had already moved through the phases of grief toward acceptance. Part of this came from me seeing the signs long before we "knew" he had autism.

From my journal entry on Dec 28, 2000 I mentioned how Nathan was really sick with a bad cold, so we prayed for him. I felt whispers from God teaching me that:

> *Nathan was such an obedient and developed man before he came to this earth that he had very little to accomplish on earth and was to be a blessing to anyone who had his acquaintance.*

What an amazing thing to learn!

Just a few months later, my mother, called to explain some of the behavioral indicators Nathan was expressing, as Tamara mentioned. She could tell he was probably autistic. Mom encouraged us to get a qualified diagnosis to "rule out" autism.

With the answers to my earlier prayers, and then the conversation with my mom, I started to see Nathan's behaviors in a different light. When he continued to regress in his vocabulary, I could finally see he had autism. This triggered me into the grieving process. I knew Nathan had special needs and that meant his development and social milestones would take him down an alternate path.

This was very sad for me. Dads have so many dreams for their sons. I struggled and grieved privately because Tamara was recovering from the accident, managing a move, and now trying to get Nathan help without acknowledging a possible diagnosis. She would look at the mounting evidence, but continued to lean toward alternate explanations, while I saw the majority of the evidence and accepted the weight of facts. Tamara was defensive to the point of being in "momma bear" mode.

I moved past denial pretty quickly, and then through shock and anger and mild depression, all on my own. I couldn't talk to Tamara about my feelings. I remember bargaining with God in my prayers, asking for a miraculous healing or something like this. In just a few months, I had moved to acceptance about two years before Nathan received his full diagnosis.

Fast forward to when we left Arkansas Children's Hospital after meeting with the diagnosis team. Tamara crashed very hard into denial, shock, and sadness. Her suffering seemed much deeper than mine. My role was to help and support her, and this was easier for me because I had already experienced all she was going through. I was able to be strong for her.

Then I started to experience her anger and frustration with me, in part, because I wasn't in

> her grieving cycle with her. At the time she started lashing out at me, I was shocked and saddened, but tried to not take it personally. These feelings were generated from the loss of our dreams for Nathan.
>
> Tamara knew Nathan had autism now and was determined to find any fix or cure possible. Again, she was wide open to any possibilities, while I tended to gravitate to the more mainstream therapies and services. We would discuss any options and would test alternative solutions in tandem with educational programs. Tamara's strength is in considering all options.

I didn't understand why Justin had already come to terms with the diagnosis. I felt like I needed to work as if everything depended on me and pray as if everything depended on God. So, I felt I had to try *everything* to fix my son . . . gluten-free/casein-free diet, many different supplements and techniques. You name it; I tried it, or at least thought about trying it. Like a ship without an anchor in the middle of a storm, I tossed every which way searching for an answer, because I didn't know which technique would "heal him."

I was begging God to send me back to Egypt. I was pleading because I didn't want this life I was now facing—at the edge of the Red Sea. Nor did I want to go through the wilderness on the other side.

My poor husband! We were both grieving in our own ways. I assumed he was processing all of this just like I was, when in reality, he had progressed beyond where I was because he sensed and acknowledged clues I didn't recognize for what they were. *Different people process diagnosis differently*—and that is okay. Some whip through it quickly and move on to acceptance. Others dally around in denial for way too long (like me), willing the diagnosis to be something else and fighting it once it is made. Therefore, patience and communication are crucial before, during, and after diagnosis.

I was too stubborn to leave the anger stage behind so quickly. Anger fueled *my will* to find a way to heal my son.

Most of all, though I hate to admit it, I blamed God and had an angry heart. I knew He could heal Nathan, and I couldn't understand why He wouldn't. I was mad because God was ruining *my life* and *my plan.* I know this sounds harsh, but I am telling this story as it really happened. I tried to bargain with Him, "I will live better, read my scriptures more, serve more, and pray more. I will do *anything*—just heal Nathan!"

I was stubborn and proud. I didn't even want to think about the possibility that perhaps autism was in God's plan all along. I wasn't humble because I wanted *my will,* not His will. Surely wanting Nathan to be healed wasn't a bad thing. Why couldn't I convince God of this?

Just because I was mad at God doesn't mean I stopped talking to Him. I talked and prayed and vented every frustration, every difficult situation, every pain, heart-ache, sorrow—I emotionally vomited it all on God.

Poor God! I'm sure He saw me as a tantruming

child whose "normal" dream had been taken away. It was as if I was banging on the "normal" door of life which had just been closed to me. I wanted to walk through that door. I wanted to have a normal family.

I was going back to Egypt. I was going to climb the cliff or find some creative solution to get there. The problem is, I was stuck because I couldn't climb my way out alone and God didn't want me to go back. He wanted me to "go forward." He knew that the promised land he had in mind for me far exceeded the shallow pleasures of Egypt.

What I couldn't understand or visualize was the "promised land" God was leading me towards. God's plan required I go a different route than I had ever imagined and through a wilderness for many years—years that would refine me.

And so as I wept in a dead end corner, God finally showed me it wasn't a dead end after all. It was a detour. *A detour is never a dead end with God on your side.*

> "And Moses said unto the people, Fear ye not, stand still, and see the salvation of the Lord, which he will shew to you today . . .
>
> And the Lord said unto Moses, wherefore criest thou unto me? Speak unto the children of Israel, that they *go forward . . .*"[7]

Then, because Moses had "cried" unto Him, God taught Moses what he needed to do to get out of the

7 Exodus 14:13, 15

dead end: "Lift thou up thy rod, and stretch out thine hand over the sea and divide it: and the children of Israel shall go on dry ground through the midst of the sea."[8]

Moses himself wondered what to do. *After he asked, God told him* how he was going to get out of the dead end. This is the key! When we pray, it is great when we talk, but it is *more important that we listen*. I think I was so busy grieving, I was doing most of the talking about *my will*. I had to learn to listen and hear God tell me how I was going to "go forward."

> "And Moses stretched out his hand over the sea; and the Lord caused the sea to go back by a strong wind all that night, and made the sea dry land, and the waters divided."[9]

That was the answer: go forward, take this new and scary path you never knew was there—straight through the middle of the sea. It is a detour, not a dead end. Have faith, take one step and then the next towards the promised land.

Confession: I have never walked through a sea. It sounds scary to me, but when the alternative is death by Egyptians, I am sure the Israelites took one step at a time until they had crossed an insurmountable obstacle.

This same lesson applied to me. I had to take baby steps of faith away from my normal expectations—away

---

8 Exodus 14:16

9 Exodus 14:21

from Egypt. It was scary and hard and I know I dragged my feet a little. No, I dragged my feet a lot!

JUSTIN: This is so true! We always comment that our life has been an experience in walking to the edge of darkness. We don't know where the path is going, and it is so frustrating! I really don't like it and if I had my way, I'd have a huge spotlight shining miles ahead on my life path. But that isn't what God's plan looks like. Let me explain this concept another way.

Have you ever seen the movie *Indiana Jones and the Last Crusade*? It's a classic and I feel no concern sharing a spoiler to anyone that hasn't seen it yet. You've had a few decades to watch it. So, in the movie there is a scene where Indy needs to traverse an impossibly huge gap between two mountains. From the side Indy was on, the cave was adorned with an epic lion's head carving. The other side was just a cave looking opening. The cliffs are sheer drop offs and no human could jump this space. I'd bet it is thirty feet wide. He must get to the other side. Lives depend on it.

Then he remembers the cheat code his dad gave him before the journey. "Only in the leap from the lion's head will he prove his worth." In this challenge, Indy would have to take a "leap of faith" across a huge canyon. In Hollywood dramatic fashion, he closes his eyes, puts out his foot and takes a large step into the empty space . . . and steps onto a hidden path that is only painted to look like a deep chasm. Yay!

It is a classic scene, and the object of the challenge was for a person to believe they can cross the impossible gap, whether they can see the path or not. And so, our life continues. And so, I continue to struggle forward.

Moving On

In a moment of undeserved mercy God gave me a recurring dream, which I eventually asked Him to stop—not because it was scary, but because I was so sad when I woke up and found the dream wasn't real.

In my dream, Nathan was talking and laughing and communicating normally with me. It was as if nothing was wrong with him. It was as if autism was the dream. My joy in the dream was immensely tangible. I talked to—really talked to and played with my boy. I can still close my eyes and picture my son in that dream because I had it so frequently, it seemed to be burned into my permanent memory. I loved that dream!

And then I'd wake up. And as the blissful dream slipped from my mind and reality hit, I cried. I grieved. I mourned—again, and again, and again, with each ensuing dream. Finally, I asked God to take the dream away because the trauma of waking up and grieving each morning was too painful for my mama heart to handle.

I haven't dreamed about my "normal" Nathan since.

You might consider me weak. I am sorry I was not strong enough to dream. The reality was too harsh each morning. I am stronger now, but not strong enough to pray for the dreams to come back.

With this dream, God helped me begin to turn my anger toward the next step of acceptance. Because, the dream planted the seed of hope that someday—maybe not in this life—Nathan will be normal in an eternal promised land. In that day when the resurrection touches all of us, this innocent soul I have been blessed to raise will finally receive a perfected body, no longer afflicted by autism.

In that day, I will finally get to see that dream become a reality. I can hardly wait for that dream to come true, when I will ultimately communicate with my Nathan and we will laugh and talk like everyone else. We won't be hampered by autism anymore. Any I won't have to wake up and see it all disappear.

DEPRESSION AND ACCEPTANCE: Following the initial diagnosis, I woke up daily feeling as if there was a heavy weight called "autism" weighing on my chest. I pushed through the raging emotions because I had to. I was a young mother with children who needed me from sunup to sundown and sometimes in the wee hours of the night. It was a full-time job. I was wandering through the wilderness.

So every day, despite the weight on my chest, I would get up and feed, and bathe, and clothe, and entertain my children. I'd wipe faces, clean messes, drop my sweet Nathan off at his special preschool and hope some therapy (especially speech therapy) would help. I prayed morning, night, and in between to get me through the day.

Through prayer I soon realized something very important: I still had my little Nathan and he hadn't changed with the diagnosis. He was still my little boy.

Regardless of his diagnosis, I was still going to love him. He was my son.

I learned something important that day: *A diagnosis doesn't define a person.* My son, was first and foremost "Nathan." The diagnosis didn't change who he was. I learned it was important to see people for who they are—not the labels affixed to them. The diagnosis was simply a way for professionals to name and properly treat an issue my son was experiencing.

I had little time to dwell in this "depression" stage. It took me a long, tough year (instead of forty years for the Israelites) to process everything and finally come to an acceptance that Nathan did indeed have autism.

Although I had accepted this fact, the "peace" of acceptance had not yet settled upon my soul. The true acceptance took a bit longer, as I had a bit more sorrow to wade through.

Throughout the diagnosis experience, I learned several important lessons:

1. Expectations are powerful dreams which are hard to replace when shattered.
2. God can turn dead ends into detours.
3. God's goal is to help us improve and get to the promised land, but we have to walk through the wilderness first.
4. Going through the cycle of grief is normal and it takes time. Be gentle to yourself and patient with others walking the same path.
5. Go forward, trudge through each day and repeat until you make it to the other side.

As a teenager, I had a friend share a scripture with me that helped me understand this concept a little better. Romans 8:28 says, "And we know that all things work together for good to them that love God." To me, this meant no matter what the situation or how it came about, God could help it all turn out for our good.

God sees what I can become when I finally reach the promised land. And, being God, He knows the best way to turn me into the person He knows I can become. But in order for that to happen, I must spend time in my own personal wilderness. The thing I learned passing through the wilderness was that you can rail against it, or you can embrace it as a gift—a purifying experience that will refine your character, strengthen your faith, deepen your bonds with God, family, and friends, and in the end, give you hope.

TRUE FAITH— WHEN THE MIRACLE YOU PRAY FOR DOESN'T HAPPEN

"FAITH IS THE ASSURANCE of things hoped for, the evidence of things not seen."[10] Faith is a belief in God and His promises even though we cannot "see" Him. Faith is often reassured through feelings, impressions, or whispers from heaven.

To me, true faith means relying completely on God, meaning you trust He can see the end from the beginning and understands *all* things. True faith is knowing He loves unconditionally and helps mercifully and faithfully in good times and bad. The hard part of learning

10 Hebrews 11:1

true faith occurs when the miracle you pray for doesn't happen—even and especially when what you are praying for is a good thing. True faith is believing in God even when things don't work out the way you want. This requires a higher level of trust in God and His will and is always easier to talk about than it is to do.

Speaking of doing, another part of true faith is a combination of action and commitment. When you have faith, you commit to fully being on God's side no matter what. You will keep going to church no matter what awful thing is happening in your own life or in the lives of those you love. For me, this was particularly heart-wrenching as we faced a life-long diagnosis. You may find yourself wondering, as I did, where God was in this awful life detour.

My journey of acquiring true faith was quite difficult. Moses told the Israelites, "Fear not: For God is come to prove you."[11] Truly these next few years were the "wilderness" of my life where God did indeed "prove" me as He did the Israelites.

Would I stay true and keep believing in Him if I had one son on the autism spectrum? What about two? How would I react then? Would I just give up, shake my fist at God and turn my back on Him or would I humble myself and submit to His will?

Diagnosis #2—Another Test of Faith

When we took Nathan to the developmental center which diagnosed him with autism, I was still nursing

11 Exodus 20:20

Jacob, our third son. At the time, Jacob was about seven months old and the diagnosing physician pointed out Nathan didn't give me eye contact like little Jacob did. Little did we know . . .

As Jacob grew, his eye contact became less frequent, he lined up cars, and had a speech delay. I convinced myself he was just imitating Nathan's behavior and I wanted the reason for Jacob's speech delay to be from his ear problems.

Tamara's Journal, February 10, 2005

Jacob has been doing well in speech therapy. I am very proud of him. He is starting to ask more for things he wants. It is such a relief to have him speaking more. It has been hard to have only one of my four children speaking.

I still worry about him. His eye contact isn't as good as I would like it to be. On occasion, the thought overwhelms me he might be on the Autism Spectrum. In those moments I feel my heart will burst with sorrow. But, I keep hoping and praying for the best. I can't lose faith he can overcome his challenges.

Tamara's Journal, April 08, 2005

Jacob has started to show more autistic symptoms like following objects with his peripheral vision. He paired two words together on his own last week "help train." He wanted me to help him fix his train. So, one step forward, two steps back.

I had a heart to heart with Justin last weekend. I poured out my heart and cried because I didn't want Jacob to be autistic. I wept because I didn't want Jordan to have another autistic brother. How I just wished we could have a "normal" family. I really do love my husband. He is wonderful and is such a support to me.

Tamara's Journal, June 12, 2005

There are mornings like this morning when I wake up and watch Jacob and say to myself, "He is autistic." Then my heart is so heavy. I pray and pray for help and strength.

Today, I walked outside and it was a beautiful and perfect morning. It was quiet except for the birds chirping and I just sat and felt the breeze. Soon I got up and went and looked at my peach trees, apple trees, blackberries, the grapevine overgrowing everything, and my garden. I don't know why, but the green things in this world bring me peace. I love being out in my garden. I wish I could spend more time there. After being outside and communing with God and nature I felt better inside.

Jacob went to the fridge today and said, "want apple." Hurray! This was a two-word sentence he put together on his own. I am encouraged!

Tamara's Journal, July 20, 2005 (Day from Hell)

I had Jacob in for his physical today. Our doctor confirmed he has autistic tendencies and I felt like crying. I know he does, but I really don't want to do this again. I don't want to lose another sweet boy to autism. It is too hard and too painful.

Autism is such a cruel disease! The baby is born and you look at it and it is so perfect. The baby develops normally and then little by little that baby is taken away…and you deny it is happening, but something is wrong. And all of a sudden, the baby that loved you will not look at you or talk to you and they start doing weird things. And you want to just weep.

Oh, how unfair life is for them, too. They get a faint glimmer of normalcy before this crippling power overtakes their mind. I hate autism. I hate it. It is destroying my children. Why does this have to happen to our family?

Tonight, I got mad and frustrated. Nathan played in his poop and wiped it all over himself two times today. Then after I had put them down for the night, Jordan yelled through their bedroom that Nathan had pooped on the floor.

When I walked in, Nathan was smearing his poop into the carpet with his foot. It was the worst I had ever seen. I just started crying and crying. I was angry. I kept saying, "Why do you do this?"

Justin has been sick today and he came upstairs and brought me the cleaning stuff—rags and a spray. The problem was it was so smeared into the carpet it wouldn't come out with a rag. I was totally overwhelmed and just kept crying.

I was angry because I didn't want to clean up the poop. The task seemed so daunting. Why would anyone play in their own poop? I was angry because I can't have a normal family. I was angry because other people have all normal kids. Sometimes, I feel like God is punishing me because I am not good enough or patient enough. Maybe God knew I wouldn't be a good enough mother and so he gave me kids I couldn't mess up.

There are times I really love being a mother and there are times I really hate being a mother. At this moment I did not like Nathan at all—I have never felt so angry with Nathan. He has been such a pill this summer. I try to help him and he yells at me. I try to get him dressed and he screams and kicks me.

Tonight after I put him in the shower and rinsed him off, I went to get him and he had stuck his fingers up his anus and smeared poop all over himself again. I was so angry. I yelled, "What is wrong with you?" This is not normal behavior. I mean, I know he isn't normal, but that is not normal for an autistic kid, is it? I guess the question is more what is wrong with me? Why do I have these feelings of anger? It isn't normal. This isn't me.

I got a counselor's name from our family doctor today. Justin and I have been talking about going to one.

I am sorry, but I had to vent tonight. I have had a headache all day, and now I feel like crap. I have apologized to everyone. I feel totally numb inside right now. As I have written this journal entry tonight I have cried again—but now I am just exhausted and numb.

Looking back at my younger self, I wish I could go back and explain those feelings of anger were part of the grieving process—and yes, it was totally normal. No, it wasn't that God was punishing me or my children. I can see now the flaws in that line of thinking. When hard stuff happens, it's human nature to try to make sense of it. And often, we wind up with completely erroneous conclusions.

God doesn't punish us like this. He loves us deeply, and He desires the brightest and best things for us, both in this life and in eternity. Even when we make mistakes or deliberate wrong choices, God doesn't punish us, nor does he hurt other innocents to make us "pay" for anything. That doesn't mean that our mistakes are without consequences. But many times in life (perhaps most times) things that go horribly awry or heart-breakingly wrong come because of the laws of nature or the result of someone else's choices. In those times, God is with us, weeping over our pains, wrapping us in His love, sending courage, hope, inspiration and strength to face our trials. We just need to remember this when faced with poopy carpet scenarios—no matter how "crappy" life seems to be. God is there to help us muck through it and come out on top.

As I look back, I know I hadn't come to the complete peace of acceptance before Jacob showed signs of autism. Going through the grieving process one more time seemed compounded the second time around. These years in my "wilderness" were full of more tears, more shattered dreams, more grieving, more wondering *why* I couldn't just have a normal family. There was more anger at myself, God, my situation and the insufficient control I seemed to have in my life.

I was struggling to understand why God wouldn't answer my prayers to heal my boys. It was a good thing to pray for, wasn't it? I had been taught since I was little to "Ask and ye shall receive."[12] Why wasn't it working? What was I lacking? More faith? More action?

> **JUSTIN:** I really wanted God to miraculously heal Nathan as well. I remember daydreaming that Nathan was healed, completely verbal, and engaging in conversations easily. Then, I could go around like the invalid healed at the Pool of Bethesda by Jesus, proclaiming how God had shown his power.[13]
>
> I have seen God's healing power many times and I've felt his Holy Spirit verify when those events are His will. When I prayed to ask for Nathan's healing, the answer came that God's will was for Nathan to continue as he was. At the time, these kind of answers made little sense to a desperate dad.

But If Not

Around this time, I heard a message which helped me understand true faith a little better. The story of Shadrach, Meshach, and Abed-nego was related from the Old Testament. I remembered the story from my

---

12 John 16:24

13 John 5:1-15

youth: Daniel and his three faithful friends were taken from their homes in Jerusalem when the Babylonians besieged it.

King Nebuchadnezzar later issued the decree that all people should bow down and worship his idols. Shadrach, Meshach, and Abed-nego refused to bow down. The king told them, if they did not, he would have them thrown into the fiery furnace.

I love the response they gave King Nebuchadnezzar,

> "If it be so, our God whom we serve is able to deliver us from the burning fiery furnace, and he will deliver us out of thine hand, O king.
>
> *But if not,* be it known unto thee, O king, that we will not serve thy gods, nor worship the golden image which thou hast set up."[14]

These brave men knew God had the power to save them just as I knew God had the power to heal my boys. Here is the difference: the "*but if not*" clause. They knew even though God could save them, perhaps He wouldn't. And, even if He didn't, they would still believe and trust in God. That is true faith and belief!

This concept hit me so powerfully because I had never thought about faith in this way! I had always believed if I was good and faithful enough, God would take away this trial . . . heal my boys—make them well. I had never understood the "but if not" clause: *If* He *didn't* heal them, would *I still believe*? Would I still trust, or would I give up on Him?

---

14 Daniel 3:17-18

The end of the story of Shadrach, Meshach and Abed-nego ends happily. God did indeed save them in the fiery furnace. In fact, when they were thrown into the furnace, the guards saw, *"four men loose, walking in the midst of the fire, and they have no hurt; and the fourth is like the Son of God."*[15]

Amidst their trial of faith, Shadrach, Meshach and Abed-nego came to know God—literally. What an awesome story!

When I heard this story, I had yet to reach this point with my faith. I still wanted my boys healed. I realized quite blatantly that I could *not* say, "God I know you can heal my boys, *but if not* I will be okay." *Because I wasn't okay with it!*

I learned that day what I was missing: greater, truer faith. I learned God did indeed have the power to heal my boys, but perhaps for some reason I couldn't comprehend, He wouldn't heal them.

Would living with this challenge test me, make me stronger, better? Probably.

Did I want to do it? No. Really. I did not.

Please God! It would be easier if you just healed them.

There were nights so dark and lonely, I just felt overcome by my grief. I wondered why I was wandering this lonely road when the sun seemed to be shining for everyone else. I wondered why I was climbing this dark and treacherous path where I felt like I was constantly stumbling and falling. How could God let this happen to me? Why was my journey so difficult to navigate?

---

15 Daniel 3:25

Why couldn't I walk the sunshiny path which seemed so much easier? Why couldn't my kids just learn to talk and converse normally? Why were social skills so challenging?

Potty training? Oh . . . don't even mention it, because my kid was 6-years-old and still didn't poop in the potty—no, he smears it on himself, and the couch and in the carpet.

When we go places, people stare. We are different and it is hard. It is a bitter pill to swallow.

God, where are you?

The answer seemed to echo back to me from a long time ago when I read an article just out of high school which taught me, "the greater the resistance, the greater the strength." God knew I was strong, but He also knew what I could become: *stronger*. So, I had to go through some resistance training.

When people lift weights, they tear their muscles and then while they rest, their amazing body builds that muscle back thicker and stronger.

That is what was happening to me emotionally and spiritually. I was trudging up my autism mountain. I was broken, weak, exhausted, drained, and bleeding. Thank goodness God knows what to do with broken things, "He healeth the broken in heart and bindeth up their wounds."[16]

God, I could use a little binding. Oh, and my heart is broken—actually, shattered. Maybe I need a new one because I don't know if you can fix my old heart and those old

16 Psalms 147:3

dreams.

And ever so slowly as I poured all my grief out to God, He began to bind my wounds. The crazy thing about walking uphill for so long is now I was stronger. I also had an added vista—because all that trudging had eventually brought me to a small summit in my wilderness. I could see things I hadn't seen before.

God took the shattered pieces of my heart and made me a pieced-together new heart and new dream. He gently helped me to realize this new vision of my life wasn't so awful. I still had my sweet Nathan and my crazy but endearing Jacob. They had a wonderful and caring older brother who was full of energy and life, and a pink bundle of joy to round off the rowdy boys.

Sure, life wasn't what I originally envisioned. But, I had to look for the blessings instead of the sorrows. I had to find things to be grateful for.

Most importantly, I learned 1) I needed to have true faith in God. This meant I had to trust Him completely, and modify my dreams and expectations, and believe He had better dreams, grander vistas, and different expectations for me. 2) I had to pray that God would change my heart and mind to parallel His will. This change of heart did not happen overnight. It happened gradually as I adjusted to the reality of my situation. Slowly, like sands dropping through a sieve one by one, my faith grew.

I learned the answer to the statement, "Ask and ye shall receive."[17] God has many blessings he is willing

---

17 John 16:24

to give us that are contingent upon our asking. But he doesn't give us everything we ask for. Can you imagine how spoiled we would be if that happened? Sometimes God's answer is immediately "yes," but other times we have to wait for an answer. And then there is the "no" answer. God doesn't answer some prayers because it is not according to His will. Those are the hardest, because it often means we are in for some spiritual learning or growth.

I learned the "no" answer, in my case, meant I was going to have to humble myself and submit to God's will. I had to come to understand true faith. Looking back, it is a lesson I am now thankful to have learned—although it wrenched my very heart-strings and I hated every minute of it at the time.

> **JUSTIN:** Faith is a spiritual muscle. And having a companion spotting you during a workout is much better and more effective and safer. Husbands and fathers . . . be the workout companion your wife needs, spiritually! Pray with her. Read the scriptures with her. Do this together with your families! You will build your faith together with God.

I can't point to a single moment when my heart began to heal, but the day did come when I could truly tell that my heart was lighter, my trust in God more secure. As for my hopes and dreams, I had once thought trusting in God meant abandoning them, but line upon line, He taught me that when we put our faith in God, when we make Him the shepherd of our dreams, they don't become diminished. Instead, we end up with blessings and outcomes that exceed our original dreams.

In order for that to happen, we must willingly choose to put our trust fully in God, like those three young men standing before the fiery furnace did. In exercising our agency by committing ourselves to God, our faith grows. Just like Indiana Jones, we must take that leap of faith before we see the fruits of that faith. Faith always precedes the miracle, but the amazing thing is that once you put your faith in God, He always blesses you, which in turn strengthens your faith further.

That one little step can seem so hard at the beginning. Like Indiana looking down into a deep abyss, it can be terrifying to take that leap. But God's promises are sure. I know because I can honestly say He healed my broken heart and helped me be truly grateful for my amazing children, a loving husband, and a wonderful life. Still, nothing of value comes quick or easy, so don't give up after one prayer or one day. God was slowly healing my heart, but I still had lessons to learn.

NOT MORE THAN WE CAN HANDLE?

I HAVE LOVED LIVING in the South for much of my married life. The people there are warm and friendly, and willing to openly talk about God, challenges they are currently facing, and life in general. While living in the South, this scene replayed many times in my life: I would be chatting with a friend and my children with autism would come up. By the end of the conversation, they would comment, "Just remember, God doesn't give us more than we can handle."

One day, as I thought about this statement, and it occurred to me, "Oh yes, *He does give us more than we can handle,* because I am not handling life well right now!" I felt overwhelmed (again).

As I sat there thinking about God "not giving more than we can handle," I realized this statement is not entirely true. Of course, He does give us more than we can handle! I believe we are here on earth to learn and be "proven" as He told the Israelites, and to see where we will turn in times of trial.

Zombie Mom

Have you ever gone through the day like a zombie because you didn't get enough sleep? You feel empty inside and your brain power is at about 20% of its normal capacity. Now, imagine doing this every single day for several years. Welcome to autism world! Zombie mom = a mom who can't handle much, but she must.

God, it's me again. I am so exhausted and can't think straight. Help me survive this day!

I don't know why kiddos on the autism spectrum don't sleep well. That is a common pattern for these children. I have come to the belief it is hard for them to calm their brains enough to go to sleep, and on top of that, any little thing seems to disturb their sleep—the weather, the fullness of the moon, or even their diets.

I know, you think I am crazy . . . but ask any Special Ed teacher or the parents of children on the spectrum about how the barometer and the phases of the moon affect their children and I am *sure* you will get an earful. These kids are more sensitive—to even things we don't perceive. So, little things affect them.

My journals are so full of week after week of lack of sleep for so many years there is no way I would include all of them. Here is just a small sample:

Tamara's Journals

September 5, 2001—Good day except the kids got up at 4:30 am!

January 26, 2002—I have been tired today. I slept in until 8:30 because Justin got up with the kids at 5:00 am. I have gotten up early all this week with the kids and I guess my body was just exhausted.

October 27, 2003—Jacob is teething and was up for about three hours before we finally got him a dose of Motrin. Then Nathan woke up, then Jordan and it was 4:15 am. Needless to say, Justin and I have been tired today.

May 22, 2004—I got to sleep in until 7:00 am because Justin got up with the kids today an early birthday present. It was so nice! Jacob woke up at 4:00 am.

July 2, 2004—Jacob was up at 3:30 am with a wet diaper which had soaked through. He did go back to sleep but Jordan was up early at 5:15. I have been tired and feeling a little "blah" today. Overall it was a good day. Justin took half the day off and we both got a nap. We have not had good sleep this week. Early wakeup calls by the boys every day.

July 6, 2004—Jordan slept in until 7:38 this morning. I know it is quite the shock any Anderson boy could sleep in that late. WOW! Don't worry, the other two were up at 5:00 am just to ensure mom and dad couldn't sleep in.

July 22, 2004—Nathan slept in until 7:30 this morning. I can't even remember the last time he slept in late!

August 6, 2004—(8 months pregnant) Sometimes I don't write in my journal because I am so exhausted at night and I feel I can hardly think and remember what happened that day. This afternoon I was dragging even after a rest.

September 27, 2004—Justin left this afternoon to go to Kansas City for some Sales Training. It was a hard night with Noelle last night. I hope she does better tonight. Justin will be glad to sleep through the night in a hotel room (poor guy)!

February 26, 2006—Yesterday we flew to Houston after a three-hour sleep since Jacob woke up around 3:00 am.

March 15, 2006—Busy day the kids woke up around 5:00 am.

Not more than I can handle? Absolutely! I was completely zombified with exhaustion!

JUSTIN: Don't tell anyone, but if there was a legal tranquilizer dart gun for kids, I would have bought one years ago! I've also imagined using the special move that Spock does to people on *Star Trek* (called "the Vulcan nerve pinch") where with one squeeze on the shoulder, they drop into unconsciousness. How sweet would that be! Unfortunately, both were fictional solutions to our sleep deprived problems.

I stumbled upon the scripture about the idea of "not giving us more than we can handle." It is found in 1 Corinthians 10:13, "But God is faithful, who will not suffer you to be *tempted* above that ye are able." The word "tempt" here comes from the Greek word *peirazō,* which means, "to test, tempt."

From what I understand, God doesn't "tempt" us. That is the devil's role. God does try us or test us, though, to prove our character. So, this verse would be more accurately translated from the Greek if it read, "But God is faithful, who will not suffer you to be *tested* above that ye are able."

Can you imagine going to school and taking the same exact test weekly for an entire school year? Boring! Where is the growth or the learning there? The same applies to life! I believe we are here to have our characters and our very natures proven. So, life won't be easy or "normal." Sometimes it will be hard, difficult, sleep-deprived and soul wrenching. But, just as a pendulum swings back and forth, there will be times of joy, happiness, and hopefully a lot of *fun*!

I love the statement from Job 23:10, "When he hath tried me, I shall come forth as gold." Wow! Isn't that awesome? What a promise. Job was tried and tested and tempted, and he did come forth as gold. Let me tell you, when I was exhausted, I would have laughed at this scripture and would have told God, "I'm good being silver instead of gold if it means I get more sleep."

So, going back to what we can handle. I think the phrase needs to be changed to say, "God doesn't give us more than we can handle *with His help.*" Basically, He doesn't give us more than *He* can handle. The question is, do we turn to Him for help in our trials?

"But God is faithful, who will not suffer you to be [tested] above that ye are able; but will with the [test] also make a way to escape, that ye may be able to bear it."[18] This verse explains God is faithful and will help us "escape" or "bear" our tests. It doesn't say He will *always* help us escape them or make them go away, although this might happen sometimes. Other times, He strengthens us to bear the tests and trials heaped upon us. Another verse I love is found in Philippians 4:13, "I can do all things through Christ which strengtheneth me." This is my mantra!

One night Nathan was up around 2:00 am and Justin and I didn't sleep well because we were taking care of him. The problem was he didn't calm down as he usually did. It was awful! He screamed and screamed and wouldn't be consoled. I don't know why. Justin and I rotated in and out of his room, "Tag. You're it. I can't take it anymore."

Finally, I set to pleading to God with sobs. Mind you I had been praying all night, but after so many hours you reach a point of desperation. *God. We have tried everything and nothing is working tonight. I don't know what to pray for, but we need help. We need angels.*

I suddenly remembered learning I needed to pray specifically for what I need. And so I began, "Please send Nathan's Grandpa Anderson, Great-Grandma and Grandpa Klein . . ." and I went on and on listing my grandparents, great-grandparents (on both sides) and every deceased ancestor I could think of, begging

---

18 1 Corinthians 10:13

and pleading they would come and help me endure and help calm Nathan.

It ended up being one of the most spiritual experiences of my life. I never saw the angels, but I felt them. There was a peace in that room which finally calmed Nathan. I know skeptics might criticize, but I will tell you I have no doubt there were angels in that room with Nathan and me.

God turned my nightmare into one of the most peaceful events of my life. I felt loved by so many of my ancestors who have "passed on." I knew I wasn't alone. God and His angels were there beside me on one of the darkest nights of my life.

> **JUSTIN:** This works! If you are on God's path and have the faith to call on angels for help, they will come. I remember when Tamara had this experience. It hadn't dawned on me to try this, but when she prayed, I felt a calming presence come help us. It was very real and it seemed to speak to Nathan's heart in a way that I couldn't understand.
>
> We have called on angels to help us since then and taught our children to do the same. There are many accounts in the scriptures of angels providing comfort, but the one I like most is from the New Testament when Jesus was suffering for the sins of the world and prays for help, "Father, if You are willing, take this cup from Me. Yet not My will, but Yours be done." Then an angel from heaven appeared to Him and *strengthened Him*."[19]

19 Luke 22:22-23

As with most people, some of my days are better than others. But at those moments when my patience wears thin, and I feel I will completely fall into the "loony bin," I have found by saying one of those silent, pleading prayers of desperation, I somehow get through the day much better. Those are the times when God sends His heavenly angels to comfort, calm, and help when we cannot do it on our own. I have had it happen too many times to deny God answers my desperate pleas for patience and peace in times of stress.

In the Sermon on the Mount, Jesus Christ taught, "*Ask*, and it shall be given you; *seek* and ye shall find; *knock* and it shall be opened unto you. For every one that asketh receiveth; and he that seeketh findeth; and to him that knocketh it shall be opened."[20]

Survival Mode

There are times when you trudge through in survival mode for a long time and you beg and plead for God to help you make it through. Even "with His help," the challenges you face day in and day out are so physically and mentally taxing that you cannot even do more than survive. It is like you are at war and it is a battle to survive.

What do you do with a child that has zero fear and has autism? You pray daily that he will live to see the age of five. Jacob was my child that gave me the most gray hairs. The challenge was that Jacob was so physically active and capable of climbing, running, and getting into things that he required a full-time supervisor.

---

20 Matthew 7:7-8

Jacob started walking at nine months and began running soon thereafter. He was determined to keep up with his older brothers. And he did. Jacob was later diagnosed with ADHD on top of autism, so you can only imagine how busy he was. I once described him in my journal as, "so sweet and so fun and so full of life and exploration of *everything*."

This is an example of two hours of one of my crazy days when Jacob was about 14 months old, Nathan was 4 ½, and Jordan was age 6.

Tamara's Journal, October 14, 2003

It was one of those evenings! The kids got into everything under the sun for the hour or two before dinner. Here is my list of crises handled:

- Picked up lids and Tupperware off the kitchen floor (again).
- Stopped Nathan from dumping dad's gel all over the bathroom, but we lost dad's chap stick—it was smeared all over the counter.
- Changed a poopie diaper.
- Explained to Jordan that "No, you can't have a friend over."
- Tried to get tantruming Nathan to go potty before he gets the computer (that was our rule).
- Changed Nathan's sandy clothes (he'd been outside in the sand box).
- Cleaned up the water Nathan had dumped on the floor.

- Had Jordan help get Jacob off the table (again).
- Cleaned up the water Jacob spilled.
- Tried to start dinner, about 20 times with interruptions.
- Phone call from Justin—He will be half an hour late.
- Stopped Jacob from falling off my dresser.
- Hid the phone from Jacob so he won't call Mongolia.
- "No Jordan, you can't play with Mitchell to-day."
- Nathan finally calms down and goes pee and goes to play the computer while Jordan watches a video (so mom can have a break).
- Explained to Jordan why we don't say, "Oh my God."
- Jacob has come with me to fix dinner so he won't turn the computer off or change the channel on the TV.
- Stopped Jacob from climbing the oven and then standing on the oven door and patting the stove burners (they were not on) . . . aga in. . . again. . . again. . .
- Memo to self: Buy latch for oven door!
- Stopped Jacob from opening dishwasher and standing on the dishwasher door.
- Stopped Jacob from banging glass bowl on cupboard.

- Set the table and put taco shells on table.
- Picked up plate off the floor and stopped Jacob from eating broken taco shell.
- Went back to making dinner.
- Crash from the other room!
- Went in and found Jacob had fallen off dining room chair, flung a glass pumpkin across the room where it shattered on the floor.
- Restrained Jacob in the high chair!
- Cleaned up glass.
- Justin comes home—Yay! Save me!

Isn't that list hilarious? I am so glad I wrote it down because I can laugh about it now. But I know that at the time I was completely frazzled by my busy boys—especially Jacob.

Having children on the autism spectrum has wrung me through the embarrassment wringer many, many times. My daily motto was *just survive*.

I learned an interesting thing in survival mode: giving God a few moments in daily prayer and scripture study allowed me to tap into his grace or enabling power. This was crucial because I was not strong enough on my own to endure or bear the challenges that were heaped upon me. I needed and begged for God's grace daily!

There were many instances where I had to beg for God to strengthen me as I passed through difficult things. For example, I've had the police called on me twice. Once, Nathan went over to a neighbor's house and walked right in. You see, this had been a friend's house, only they had just moved, so the new couple didn't know us or Nathan yet. They got to know us that day.

Tamara's Journal, September 30, 2006

This afternoon has been a bit taxing emotionally. Tonight Nathan got out. He walked down to a new neighbor's house. The guy tried to get him to talk to him, but of course Nathan doesn't exactly talk. By the time I discovered he was missing, the guy had called the cops and they were there trying to get Nathan to tell them who he was and where he belonged. (To make matters worse, he was wearing only a t-shirt and underwear—no pants.)

Thank goodness I spotted them and came running. One of the officers was nice. He has a developmentally disabled daughter, and told me that he knew how it was. They suggested that he should get a medical bracelet, so it would say who he is and where he belongs if he gets out. I honestly don't know if he would keep it on. I have been worried and prayerful all night...what if it happens again? I just feel depleted, frustrated and stressed. How am I supposed to take care of my children? I feel like I have made my home a fortress. It is hard to escape, but somehow they still manage to escape here and there.

The other time the police were called it was for Jacob. Jacob was much more of an escape artist. We had double locks on our front door, plus a little alarm. He would usually escape out the back door, hop the six-foot wooden fence (something he started doing when he was three-years-old), and run off to explore.

Tamara's letter to a family member, May 10, 2006

Jacob, well he is just my little tornado. One of the funny things he does is he goes out to the garage and climbs onto Justin's big work-out machine and then he hangs on it with his feet dangling and says "monkey." I laugh, because he is my monkey! He keeps climbing the fence too…so I have become paranoid parent every time he goes outside. On Sunday, he jumped the fence even though I kept telling him to get down. He wouldn't come to me even though I kept calling him, so I jumped the fence too (just try to imagine that if you will—Tamara scaling and falling off a 6-foot fence). I kept thinking I am going to kill my knees by dropping this far. Well, I caught him and we survived!

I did everything in my power to keep him safe. I prayed to God daily that we could keep up with Jacob, and that He would give me the wisdom to know how to do this. When Jacob used the horizontal wooden posts on the fence to help him climb, we invested in more planks and ensured that only vertical slats faced our yard. He then used to use the little red and yellow car to boost him over the fence. So, that disappeared. Then he would stack our sand toys on top of each other to boost him over the fence. So those disappeared as well. Sigh! Then he would stick his fingers in the little vertical gaps between boards to Spider-man crawl his way to the top of the fence.

Come on! Seriously! How do I keep this kid safe when he is determined to run? *Dear God, help me keep Jacob safe today*, continued to be my daily plea for help.

Tamara's letter to a family member, June 20, 2007

> Jacob . . . ah, well, can you say "Houdini?" Jacob has managed to keep learning new ways to escape from our backyard. I don't think I can count the number of times in this past month that a neighbor has brought him to the door or we have had one of those, "Oh no! Where is Jacob?" moments.
>
> Justin's dad lovingly helped us build another blockade to try to keep him in, but Jacob seems to keep a step ahead of us. I think I need to confiscate all the bikes/big wheels in the backyard that he is using to propel himself over the fence.

Usually when Jacob escaped, he ended up at what he called "604" where some good friends lived. He would just waltz right in their home like he owned the place. Our poor neighbors—no privacy. Thank goodness they were kind neighbors and I would normally get a call that sounded something like this, "Tamara. I don't want you to be worried, but Jacob is down here. He is more than welcome to stay." Sigh! I would run out the door to go and get him.

But there was that one time that he got out and "604" was locked and he spotted something very tempting at another house through a gap in the fence—a pool. So, how do you problem solve getting over their 6 foot fence? Well, Jacob went back up the street, removed the two-foot cylindrical cover off the electrical panel that they have in front yard and hauled it over to the fence to boost himself over.

Can you imagine this neighbor's heart attack when she looked out her patio window while home for lunch and saw Jacob standing at the edge of her pool? That produced another panicked call and a visit by the police. Sigh! These kiddos are going to turn me into a criminal. Survival!

I was doing everything I could to keep them safe and happy. I happened to have both a babysitter and I watching the kids that day . . . but Jacob was simply our sneaky escape artist and I had other children that needed my attention.

Can you imagine my prayers after that night? *Dear God, please help Jacob. Help him begin to develop some sliver of awareness of danger.* God did continue to bless me with ideas to help.

> **JUSTIN:** These are very serious situations and super scary. But I'd like to tell you one of my all-time favorite stories about the double escape Nathan and Jacob did one Sunday.
>
> We had gotten a decent night's sleep and we were waking up naturally around 6am. This was a sweet moment where the sun was starting to shine and I could hear the birds chirping so clearly . . . too clearly. *Why can I hear them so clearly?!* Then it hit me: the front door was open. I sprang up to investigate and confirmed the door was open, which meant someone was outside.
>
> I ran outside in my pajamas and spotted Jacob

> playing in the street gutters down at 604. There was still a bit of sprinkler water there and he was having a ball splashing in it. So, I strolled down the sidewalk to get him, having a little chuckle with myself at the fun happening so early in the morning.
>
> When I got to 604's mailbox to get Jacob, I saw something out of my peripheral vision that made me do a double take. It seemed that 604's front door was wide open! I guessed that Jacob had opened their door, so I went to close the door. That is when I did a major double take—inside their living room was my other son, Nathan. He was enjoying a stroll on their elliptical *butt naked*!
>
> I shot through the door, grabbled Nathan (I might have even put my hand on his mouth so we could avoid any noises) and hauled him out of there! Then I took each son by the hand and walked them back home, laughing the whole way. I don't even think I acted mad or upset with them. This was Anderson lore in the making!

I remember one particularly difficult family reunion up near Bear Lake in Idaho. Change is particularly hard with kiddos on the spectrum. They don't like to have their schedules altered. Due to the change of the vacation, they usually threw more frequent tantrums, did not sleep as well (which means you don't sleep as well), and in general made everyone miserable.

We have a humorous extended family photo that year of everyone smiling while Justin and I are each holding a crying and tantruming child—Jacob and Nathan. Yes, we were doing the "I am only smiling on the outside" smile in that picture, but it shows how awful life was at that moment. Mind you, every other child in the photo looks just fine. Sigh! This was our normal.

That same reunion Jacob escaped the house and went tearing down the hill towards the combine that was cutting/harvesting hay at the bottom of the hill. I screamed at him to stop while Justin, boosted by adrenaline, caught him before he reached the machinery. What . . . the . . . heck? Running toward danger.

Dear God, help me keep my boy safe today, and give me the strength to keep up with him.

Then there were the everyday occurrences that became dangerous anytime Jacob was involved. Things like getting him out of the car were dangerous. He would always unbuckle himself the second we arrived and Justin and I would have to position ourselves one at the front of the car and one at the back of the car so that we could catch him the second he bolted from the door. He would run whichever way was open—straight towards the street. Yes. It was exhausting . . . and he was only *one* of our four children.

I personally comprehend the study that came out in 2009 that stated that, when the stress levels of mothers (and I will include fathers) of autistic children were measured, they were comparable to combat soldiers. Can you see why? We are in the trenches every day—dealing with life and death situations that often induce the stress hormone cortisol. It screws up our hormones because producing that much adrenaline wears out our adrenal glands. Would it surprise you to find out that I have gone into Adrenal Fatigue at least three times since my children were diagnosed with autism? I've been battling my way back to health for many years now. It takes its toll.

I am thankful that God helped my children (including and especially Jacob) to mature, improve, and grow out of many of those perilous activities.

As a teenager, Jacob now rides his bike to friend's houses without supervision, and I don't have to worry about him or Nathan running away anymore. Nathan now keeps his clothes on and doesn't run naked down our street. Praise God they outgrew that phase! I am thankful because it was exhausting chasing them as they ran towards danger.

I don't think I would ever wish "survival mode" on anyone, but so many people all over the world live in this mode for weeks, months and years like we did. The key is relying on God's grace and His blessings of persistence and ingenuity to get us through.

God only gives us enough grace to make it through that stressful day, as we sincerely ask. Then, the next day, He does the same. He helps us moment by moment and day after day as we seek Him and plead for help during any survival mode.

God helped me endure and even survive with two young children on the autism spectrum. I learned through experience this profound truth: two people can do anything if one of them is God.

I used to think God only worked doing big miracles—like the parting of the Red Sea. But I have come to see that it is the little daily mercies that add up to big miracles—like surviving as a zombified mommy for years, or keeping Jacob alive after he ran toward danger.

I learned that a daily dose of prayer and a few moments of pondering God's word gave me the strength to make it through (I will talk about this in more depth in an upcoming chapter). These were the "action" part of true faith that allowed Him to bless me—even though I never deserved it. That is why it is called mercy or grace.

Robert Robinson, a Baptist hymn writer penned the words for "Come, Thou Fount of Every Blessing" in 1758. These words seem to express how I feel about God getting me through hell and back.

O to grace, how great a debtor, daily I'm constrained to be!

Let thy goodness like a fetter* bind my wandering heart to thee.

(*Fetter: a chain placed on the ankle of a prisoner)

I am so grateful for God's daily grace which strengthened me beyond my normal capacity, gave me wisdom beyond my own, and blessed me with angels as I struggled through my wilderness. I learned firsthand that God doesn't give you more than you can handle *with His help!*

COMPARING & COVETING

Avoiding the Comparison Trap

One of the hardest things living in this digital age is how we compare ourselves to touched-up modeled photos, immaculate houses in magazines, and the façades people post online. It is easy to get depressed thinking you will never live up to the fairy-tale digital world.

I wish I could say I never have fallen into the comparison trap, but I have—especially as I watched "normal" families right before and after Nathan was diagnosed.

I wish I could say that once I accepted Nathan's autism I never grieved again, but that would be a lie. Every class performance in elementary school where he would "sing" beside his normal peers (he actually stood off to the side with his aide and flapped his hands), my grief returned. Seeing him beside typical kids his age made his disability so apparent that I left those performances in tears, while other parents smiled brightly, proud to have seen their child on stage.

JUSTIN: The performances never bothered me. I think it is cool that people are willing to help try and integrate these special needs kids. Where I find myself grieving is when I see boys Nathan's age hitting milestones or enjoying events or socializing in a way he never will. Some examples are when I see kids playing together in a park, or a youth baseball team, or sharing a laugh. Then I think that my son can't do any of those things. You could say I fall into the comparison trap Tamara was mentioning. I guess it is natural.

At other times, the grief assailed me in different ways. I remember a friend telling me she was almost an empty nester. She described how different it would be not to have kids underfoot, and how she thought she'd transition into a different phase of life. Toward the end of our conversation, she commented, "You'll see soon enough. Kids grow up so fast!" I left the conversation grieving, because unlike her, I would never have an empty nest.

What I learned over time about these attacks of grief is that they generally hit me when I compared myself, my life, and my children with other people. I have since gained enough wisdom to avoid the comparison trap. But that only happened when I internalized being "normal for me." This acceptance came gradually, but it did come.

You might ask what happened for me to finally say I truly am "normal for me?" There were a few core principles I had to learn in my heart.

1. Know who you really are.

Who are you? Really? If I asked you this question, you might start listing your titles: Teacher, Investor, Coach, Pianist, Baker, Business-person, Accountant, Judge, Gardener, Sports-Enthusiast, etc. These are good titles to describe what we do and perhaps some of our hobbies, but they don't talk much about who we truly are.

You are the son or daughter of the most powerful being in the universe. You are a son of God or daughter of God. When you strip away every title, this is at the core of who we each are. "The Spirit itself beareth witness with our spirit, that we are the children of God."[21] As His children, we are so valuable to Him.

Another quote from the New Testament confirms this: "Know ye not that ye are the temple of God, and that the Spirit of God dwelleth in you?"[22] I believe this! I believe we are spirit children of an immortal and perfect God. This physical body we see is imperfect compared to the divine spirits that inhabit our bodies, but it is also beautiful and patterned "in His own image."[23]

These simple truths are what helped me make it through hard years as a teenager when I endured bullying and unkindness from my peers. My parents taught

---

21 Romans 8:16

22 1 Corinthians 3:16

23 Genesis 1:27

me I was a daughter of God, and He loved me no matter what everybody else thought. I learned to love the scripture in 1 Samuel 16:7 where the Lord says, "Look not on his countenance, or on the height of his stature . . . for man looketh on the outward appearance, but the Lord looketh on the heart."

Truly, we look at people's outward appearance. We shouldn't compare and judge, but we do. It is only as we get to know people better that we can catch a glimpse of who they are in their heart. Only God knows what marvelous beings we are inside, and only He can teach us, and help us know of our eternal worth and the worth of those around us.

While in high school, one of my friends, Daryl Smith, taught me a lesson about our true identity. Daryl was one of those fun people to be around. He always had a positive comment for you or a cheerful "Hello." Everyone knew and loved being around Daryl.

One day we were walking to class together when a fellow student walked by us swearing up a storm. I commented something like, "Wow! That was something else." Without missing a beat Daryl responded, "He is a child of God, too!" What an amazing lesson! What was crazy, is I had been taught I was a child of God since I was little, but I never had looked at *every* person in my high school as a child of God until that day—no matter what they looked like or dressed like or said. I suddenly realized why Daryl was so popular and well-liked. He saw everyone as children of God and treated them as such.

I have noticed women in particular (and some

men) spend too much time comparing themselves to others. We need to quit comparing ourselves to perfect images that have been touched up and made to look perfect! We must stop comparing our weaknesses to other people's strengths! We are unique and wonderful just being who we are! I believe we should all learn to be comfortable and happy in our own skin.

We don't need to dress in the latest styles to be important. God loves us simply because we are His daughters or sons. He doesn't want me or you to be a copy of our neighbor down the street. He wants each person to be the best person they can be! And so, I've decided to be the best Tamara Anderson I can be, because I could never be the best Susan or Jane or Kim (because I'm not them). The same is true for you. Be the best you that you can be. Compare yourself to your own standard and work and set goals so you can improve you.

As a teenager, I remember my dad telling me that if I ever had a bad day, and wondered if I was worth anything, I needed to pray. He encouraged me to get on my knees and ask God, *Do you love me? Am I of worth?* Then dad said I should listen with my heart, and the answer would come. I have put this to the test. I have prayed and listened in moments of doubt, and the sweetest feelings of love and comfort have filled my soul, so now I have no doubt that God knows me and loves me. I know I am His spirit daughter. I know I am of worth.

I have thought about these things regarding my boys with special needs. I believe God sent them to these physically challenged bodies for several reasons. One reason is to teach others and myself patience and true love. Another reason is because their spirits or souls are so good and so pure that He didn't want them defiled by all the wickedness pervasive in our world.

When my children were diagnosed on the autism spectrum it caused me to reevaluate my life and its purpose and meaning. It was so tempting to prioritize "earthly" titles over eternal titles. But I knew I was a daughter of God and that my sons on the spectrum were sons of God. This is what mattered in the end—not how they compared to other children their age. God valued my children just as they were. He didn't compare them to the popular or the posh. They were normal for them. What an important principle to learn and internalize.

> **JUSTIN:** When I have prayed over Nathan, I have had miraculous experiences. In our faith, we believe in the laying on of hands to give a blessing or a heartfelt prayer. When I do this, I feel like I *see Nathan as he really is* . . . a powerful, loving, faithful man. This will sound weird to some of you. Bear with me for a second.
>
> The scriptures teach us that our bodies are just a vessel for our eternal spirits. That eternal spirit is who we really are. We lived with God before we came here for who knows how long . . . millions of years. We matured and developed into a person that we don't remember. I have little understanding of who I really am as this eternal being. But for some reason, God has "opened my eyes" and

shown me glimpses of who Nathan really is.

I cannot find words to share what I've learned, but let me try. I feel a greatness about this boy I cannot explain. I'm humbled to be in the presence of greatness. I am his inferior in every way. Everything I do for him is an honor and a blessing. I feel God's love for him in such an intense and deep way that I know my son will live with God forever. I know it, and because I know it, I know I need to step up my game if I'm going to be with Nathan and God after I die.

And I think some of you will wonder how you can feel what I feel. I don't know that answer exactly for each of you, but I believe sincerely praying for this gift is a great start. It is God's gift to give, not mine.

2. Love or Coveting

I am the oldest of six children in my family. There were five girls born first, and then a boy at the tail end! All of us girls are strong-willed. Now I wonder how my parents ever survived all of us girls going through puberty. Sister number three is Lisa. Lisa and I butted heads growing up. I particularly remember us facing each other, angry as hornets, with our fists up. Yes, life in the Klein home was full of daily lessons on repentance and forgiveness. But, through it all, we did learn to love each other.

Lisa was an awesome basketball player in high school and college, and built for it too, being six feet tall, strong, competitive, and beautiful. She passed me up in height during my mission. My "little" sister had become my "big" sister. She served a mission in Chile and eventually had to come home with health challenges. The spirit was willing, but the flesh was weak. She married a wonderful man named Chris, and they have two beautiful daughters. Through it all, Lisa's health continued to decline and no doctor could tell us why.

Lisa and I have had many conversations over the years about trials. I recorded one of those chats we had in a letter dated January 10, 2008:

> Yesterday I was talking to my sister Lisa on the phone. She has suffered with chronic migraines and severe health challenges since her mission (ten years ago). I don't know how or why she has had to suffer all she has, I only know it has been a *very long and hard* road for her. She told me at many points she has felt, "Nobody knows or understands what I have gone through." After feeling this way for many years, she said one day a different thought came to her, "Do I want people to have to suffer and go through all I have gone through just to understand me?" After thinking of all her friends and loved ones she decided, no, she didn't want to have them suffer to understand.
>
> She also said she felt jealousy toward people with "normal lives." Finally, she realized she was coveting other people's normal lives, and she knew the commandment, "Thou shalt not covet," seemed to apply. Through prayer, she asked the Lord to

help her overcome these feelings of jealousy and help her feel closer to her friends and loved ones. God has blessed her and helped her, and now she is finally feeling some spiritual relief.

What amazing insight! As Lisa told me this story, I realized I, too, had been guilty of coveting, although I had never called it that. The interesting thing is God taught Lisa and me the same exact lesson through our trials. God taught us both that desiring what someone else has (to the point where you are unhappy they have it and you don't), even if it is health, normal children, talents, marriages, or whatever else—that is coveting.

Why would coveting be so serious that God prohibits it as one of the Ten Commandments? I recently looked up all the references of the word "covet" in the scriptures because I wanted to understand this concept a little better. I originally thought jealousy and ingratitude were at the root of coveting, but my study of the scriptures pointed me in another direction.

The first four of the Ten Commandments can be summarized as "Love God." I found a great scripture in Romans 13:9 where Paul lists the second half of the Ten Commandments (including the command not to covet) and then summarizes them by saying, "Thou shalt love thy neighbor as thyself." He then continues in verse 10 by saying, "Love worketh no ill to his neighbor: therefore, love is the fulfilling of the law."

Now, I had heard "love thy neighbor as thyself" many, many times throughout my life, but I guess I had never put two and two together—First, I had to learn to love God and as I did, I would love myself; and second, once I loved myself, it would then help me truly love my neighbor and not covet their children, their home, or anything else.

The more I have considered this, the more I believe it is a process which takes place gradually over time. Whatever our capacity for love towards ourselves and towards God can also be shown to our neighbor. As we learn to love God and ourselves more, our capacity to love our neighbor also increases.

So, the ultimate measurement for coveting lies in our heart. What do we love more: God and others, OR obtaining money, wealth, or power (being better than everyone else)? It seems to me that loving God and putting Him first is a key to not coveting, and loving and caring for ourselves and for those around us is just as fundamental.

Now, obviously, this concept of learning not to covet is much easier to talk about than it is to live. In my situation, I watched other families going on walks, or to the store, or sitting quietly in church, and I envied them. I wanted what they had (what I perceived as "normal" kids), and because I wanted it so badly and compared myself to them so much, I became unhappy with my own situation.

I tried my best to love my neighbor at the time, but until God taught me to love my "normal" life, I could not completely love others. Once I embraced my lot in life, only then did I become liberated from coveting and more grateful and content with the children I had. This acceptance put me back on the path of truly loving others for who they are and being less judgmental. Ultimately, it is a realization we all should make at some point or another, and I think it requires God's help to make this change. I, like Lisa, had to pray for the strength to change, and then worked with God day after day as He changed my heart.

JUSTIN: I remember being so jealous of the "normal" families at church. Since we ended up sitting near the front so our kids would be less distracted, we were also showing the congregation what terrible parents we were, or so I thought. There was one family that often sat a row or two behind us and their children sat perfectly still while ours were demonstrating what utter chaos looked like. I was not only jealous of that family, but I felt resentment towards God for the contrast between a perfect family and ours.

As we got to know that family, we learned that they were also good people and we became friends. They were sincere and empathetic to our situation and never showed any level of judgement. God helped change my heart so that I saw them as the good people that they were, and not as a standard to hold up against our family.

That doesn't mean we always feel fairly judged. Not even close! I can't number the times that people somewhere in public give us the look that says, "Do you have any clue how to be a parent?" or "Will you tell your 6 foot 2-inch man-sized son to stop yelling?" This still happens regularly, but now that we know this is "normal for us" we can usually shrug off the glares and do our best in those circumstances.

I originally believed jealousy was at the root of coveting and I realized this is the opposite of love. When we want something we don't have to the point where desire turns into coveting, that yearning eats away at our joy and we are not happy. God wants His children to be happy with the things he blesses us with. As we choose to be content and grateful for what we have, God will not only bless us with what we need, or the skills to obtain what we need, but He will bless us with the capacity to love others more perfectly (as a bonus).

All this advice may still seem a bitter pill to swallow for anyone struggling with chronic depression or any other form of mental illness. May I just say to you, God loves you! You are His precious child! He knows what you are going through. Jesus Christ himself was "a man of sorrows and acquainted with grief."[24] He has felt your pain and carried your burden.

Though you may feel desperately alone and so deep in a pit it seems like it will not get any better, God understands and invites you to "Come unto me, all ye that labour and are heavy laden, and I will give you rest."[25] Turn to Him, seek medical help, and talk to a trusted friend or neighbor. Burdens are easier when shared. Desiring to improve your situation is not coveting. God will help you find solutions to your problems or make you strong enough to bear them with His help. God will send moments of sweetness . . . even down in your pit.

---

24 Isaiah 53:3

25 Matthew 11:28

Going back to my sister Lisa. A few years ago, we finally found out she has had Lyme disease. She has been through hell and back with treatments over the past years. It has been tough! Although she is still not "better," she continues to provide us with plenty of jokes, laughter, and funny stories. Lisa has chosen to turn to God, even in moments of deep depression. Answers haven't come all at once, but she has looked for and found moments of love and joy instead of coveting and jealousy. There are still plenty of bad days, but the lessons she teaches us through her example of positively enduring her trials are amazing!

So, in the world of never-ending media images that teach us we aren't good enough or don't have the right things, remember these two lessons I learned. Comparing and coveting will not bring joy in the end. Only seeing ourselves and others as children of God will fill us with love and bring us true happiness.

Don't worry if you aren't there yet. Talk to God about your desire to learn to love Him, yourself, and your challenges. This isn't something that happens overnight. It is a gradual process. Don't get discouraged if it seems to take forever. God is in the "forever" business and He can help you just as he helped and guided Lisa and me with our "thorn in the flesh" as Paul calls it. Just like Paul, we asked God, "That it might depart from me." But God responded, "My grace is sufficient for thee: for my strength is made perfect in weakness." Paul concludes, "Most gladly therefore will I rather glory in my infirmities . . . for when I am weak, then

I am strong."[26] God can indeed help us change these comparing and coveting ailments into self-worth and love. How great it is to be free from those awful comparison traps with God's help.

I have walked this path, and I know it works. I had to turn to God and beg that he would fill me with love or charity—and take away that constant comparison, coveting, and jealousy. I'm getting better at it, though I am far from perfection. I have sensed a gradual change in my heart and soul—and I know God is at work.

God can help each of us learn to love Him, ourselves, and others more. He can help us raise our sights above earthly things and titles to see the true worth of a soul. God wants us to be happy. We just need to choose to love and pray for help.

---

26 2 Corinthians 12:7-10

MY TOOLBOX

I RECEIVED MY FIRST TOOLBOX for Christmas when I was twelve years old. I know, some of you are thinking, "What were your parents thinking giving a twelve-year-old girl a tool box?" I am not a stereotypical girl because I *loved* that toolbox! I loved fixing things around our house.

If a drawer broke, my mom would call me (dad was often at work) and I would take it apart, figure out how it worked, what was wrong, and how I could fix it. This is how my brain works. I love solving problems!

Over the years, I bought a new tool here and there to help me fix a something in the house. By the time Justin and I married, I brought a full toolbox to our first apartment.

JUSTIN: I feel like I've hit the jackpot here! Tamara still fixes a lot of things around the house, and I love it!

Toolbox of Learning

When Nathan was initially diagnosed with autism, the things I knew about autism would have fit on an index card. I felt overwhelmed thinking about this new diagnosis because I feared the unknown. Usually people fear what they don't know or understand. My autism toolbox was empty.

I began reading books about autism. I learned kids on the autism spectrum like sticking to schedules. Dang! This was a hard tool to learn because I am a bit spontaneous.

I joined an autism support group who held meetings and attended conferences that gave me "hammers," "saws," and "screwdrivers" to put in my autism toolbox. An example of one of these tools is that people on the autism spectrum are usually visual learners, so it is more effective to teach them using books, videos, or computers.

The more I learned, the more empowered I felt to "fix" or "problem solve" the challenges I faced every day raising my kids with autism. I had a toolbox now!

Using My Toolbox

Once a week our family has a "Family Night." We sing together, pray together, have a short gospel lesson, play games, and have a treat. One of the hardest things for me when my family was young was helping my children with autism participate in our special family time—so that each member of our family could truly participate.

One day a few years ago, as I prepared a short lesson

for our family night, I puzzled how to help my sons with autism participate. So I used one tool that has always worked for me: prayer. I told God I wanted to involve my *entire* family, but I didn't know how to do it. I figured my children were God's children before they were ever mine, and I asked Him to teach me what to do.

No sooner had I presented my request then thoughts and ideas came to my mind. One of the first ideas I had was to make a poster of the songs we sang so the kids could follow along. I sat down and wrote the song out. I drew little pictures as well (where appropriate) so the kids (even those who couldn't read yet) could learn the songs. Now, Nathan won't usually sing while we sing, but I discovered he would shine a flashlight on each word while we sang. That was his way of participating.

God inspired me to use the "visual learning" tool from my autism toolbox to help Nathan participate.

Another dilemma presented itself when Nathan was in middle school. He has always struggled with verbally expressing himself, and we decided to work with his teachers to improve his verbalization.

When you look into Nathan's eyes, you can see his brain working. You can see there is so much going on and so much he could say, but for some reason with his autism, there is a disconnect between thinking something and being able to say it. Can you imagine how frustrating that would be?

In my research into helping non-verbal children with autism communicate better, I stumbled upon the "tool" that some of these children did well when exposed to sign language. I tried it—even though I knew it was a long shot. At the annual goal planning meeting with Nathan's teachers that year, we coordinated a plan to teaching him a little bit of sign language through simple movies, because he learned best through visual examples. We focused on simple phrases like, "I am hungry," "I am thirsty," "I need to go potty," or "I want iPad." My husband is very good at making simple movies on the computer. With our family making the movies, we could customize them to exactly what Nathan needed to learn. We then burned the sign language movies to a DVD. These short movies taught Nathan basic words and sign language. Subsequently, we sent a copy to school, so they could reinforce what we did at home.

A miracle happened! Once Nathan learned a word by signing it, he could say it verbally even when he didn't sign it. We had found the key to unlock his communication block. His spoken vocabulary increased dramatically! We celebrated that he could now say, "I want cookie," or sign and say, "Thirsty." This was a *huge* success for my sweet ten-year-old boy!

I consider it a miracle God led me to find the right tool to effectively teach sign language to Nathan. God also paved the way for an entire team of people to help us. I am so thankful for everyone who helped. He led me to make a new friend who just "happened" to know sign language. We couldn't have done the movies without her. Then Nathan's teachers at school worked as a team, helping him to progress past the barriers which had kept him silent for too long.

JUSTIN: I really enjoy making small movies for the family. When Tamara came to me with the idea to teach Nathan words using sign language, I was thrilled to get to work. Tamara filmed a friend signing the words and phrases we wanted to teach Nathan. Then I created little segments that went something like this:

- Expert signs and says the word "bus;" various family members then sign and say "bus."
- Expert signs and says the phrase "time to go;" family members do this.
- Expert signs and says the phrase "time to go (to) bus;" family members do the same.
- Then the screen says, "Now it is Nathan's turn." Then the words and phrases show up at intervals (so Nathan can practice).
- Then we all celebrate with a big, "Great job, Nathan!"

It didn't take long for me to see that this was a brilliant idea. We would send a DVD of these to school. Teachers would show them to the entire special needs class. Pretty soon, Nathan, and most of his peers, would be either saying, or signing, these phrases. This was really funny at times because the videos were so specific to Nathan, so when all of Nathan's class could say his address or phone number, we knew these videos were effective! Some videos worked better than others, but we saw a improvement in the words Nathan would say to us.

And I got a bit crazy with this. I started theming the videos around activities or movies or whatever Nathan loved. My favorite was the *Star Wars* one where we did a lot of video in front of a green screen. Nathan still likes watching that one, primarily because I put some funny outtakes at the end of it. He still repeats the lines we messed up!

The time and effort to create these videos was so insignificant compared to the joy and satisfaction I felt when Nathan opened up a little more to us!

Another miracle occurred when we were trying to get Nathan to stay in his room until it was time to wake up. Our school district offered a class on teaching children on the autism spectrum through making social stories, and I happily attended. I knew it would add another tool to my autism toolbox.

A social story is a book you make which helps your child know what a certain situation should look like socially. The school district then gave us the opportunity to come down to the district offices for a day and use school equipment to make our social story, with specialists to help us along the way. They even had Special Education teachers there to help us with specific questions we might have. This was a fantastic addition to my autism toolbox!

I wrote a social story with pictures which talked about how Nathan needed to stay in his room until 6:00 a.m. no matter what time he woke up. We then read this little "book" nightly before bed.

Reading the book—coupled with persistence, melatonin, and noise makers—helped Nathan sleep better. And because he was sleeping better, we slept better. The miracle was, once we got Nathan sleeping better, his behavior improved dramatically. His tantrums decreased, and he seemed happier. I cannot tell you how crucial this was for our overall health, and his.

What a great tool to learn and apply with success! This same scenario can be applied to any issue—cancer, diabetes, depression, anxiety, high blood pressure, etc. Learn all you can and put tips in your toolbox of learning. Perhaps deep breathing will help when anxiety skyrockets, or painting your nails will help you keep them from falling off during chemotherapy. There are lots of tips and tricks you can learn to help with different challenges.

I had to add different tools to my mothering toolbox as I learned to juggle the demands of four children, two of whom had autism. I learned to encourage differently when Jacob always wanted to "win." I found out that saying, "Anyone who makes it to the top of the stairs is a winner" worked better than "First one to the top wins." This inevitably caused a meltdown because Jordan would win and Jacob would cry.

God is a perfect teacher if we are willing to go to him with dilemmas. Sometimes He sends friends to help us find the solutions. I have had many "light bulb moments" while talking to friends about perplexing situations in my life. Other times we've had to visit the doctor when we hit a dead end.

I have also found answers on the Internet (Google is

great!). Learning also occurred at different conferences on autism. Books are also some of my best friends! There is a world of knowledge out there to be gained, and I believe God expects us to do our part to learn, so He isn't working with a blank slate. We need to put tools of learning in our toolbox of life and then turn to God to guide us on which tool we need to use at the right time to fix whatever problem we are facing.

Now, there are some solutions you cannot find in a book, or on the Internet, or from a friend. I have found myself in that predicament many times and have learned God will often answer my prayers with the inspiration I need . . . sometimes immediately, and sometimes not so immediately. But somehow, some way, God will help us proceed and know how to keep going. He will help us solve the problems within our control and give us patience and wisdom to endure those which aren't.

So, no matter what diagnosis you are facing, fill your toolbox full of knowledge. Learn, read, take classes, discuss with specialists, and talk with others in your situation. Knowledge helps us overcome fear. When you pair your toolbox of knowledge with God, you will find solutions to the perplexing situations around you. You will learn to fix things like I learned to solve problems with my toolbox at twelve. It is empowering! Give it a try!

SUPPORT GROUP SAVIORS

Surviving any diagnosis utterly alone seems so incredibly daunting, I can barely wrap my mind around it. With any "caregiver" situation, there is a need for respite, support, and the desire to share the heavy burden with others. Perhaps a loved one is diagnosed with cancer, or a parent is diagnosed with Alzheimer's. Autism is no different.

Supportive Spouse

I realize not everyone has a supportive spouse, and my heart goes out to those who do not. God bless you with an added measure of comfort and strength!

> **JUSTIN:** Right before we married, I asked my father-in-law the secret to his long and happy marriage with his wife. I anticipated he would say something like "put your spouse first," and so I

> was surprised when his advice was, "Put God first and your spouse second and children third and everything else will fall into place." We decided to try and do this. Our marriage was tried and tested through the double-diagnosis, several moves, and health challenges. I am glad we sought out God as a partner because I don't know how we would have survived otherwise.
>
> Some of the ways I try to put God first are by making my personal worship a top priority. This includes having my own private prayers and scripture study. Another idea that helps is to be active in your church or local men's groups and take advantage of opportunities to serve others. This focus is just as critical for those without a spouse to significant other. Have God be your partner in your trials. He is much more capable than any of us.

Justin and I prioritized going on frequent dates. We scheduled this almost weekly, got a babysitter, and went. This was essential! It was a great get-away for Justin and me to have a break from the high stress of chasing children and focus on each other for a few hours. We got a chance to talk about how things were going, how we were doing, laugh, and reconnect. Dating was non-negotiable!

Tamara's Journal, January 26, 2002

Justin and I went on a date tonight dinner and a movie. It is always nice to be with him. He has been on three business trips this month and we found out he has to take another one this week. I am sad about that. I don't like to have him gone because he is such a help and support to me.

Tamara's Journal, July 16, 2004

We went on a fun date tonight to play games at a friend's home. We played "The Not So Newlywed Game." It was fun and we laughed a lot. I am married to quite the character! I sure love him though.

Tamara's Journal, November 28, 2004

We went on a double-date with Justin's sister and her husband. First, we went to a second-hand store where we had to pick out a gift for our spouse for under $5.00. Justin got me this sexy Santa lingerie (we all laughed). He is such a stinker!

I got him some comedic books on "Love and Marriage" and getting old. Jen got roller blades and Tyler got books and a aco holder. Then we went out to eat and told stories about our college days and the pranks we all played. We just laughed and laughed.

I know some of you are thinking that going on dates frequently had to be expensive. We didn't go on super-expensive dates. We took advantage of local productions at the junior highs, high schools, and universities. Sometimes we would take a walk together or do the shopping together (without kids it was a treat). We didn't have much extra money. But we did budget for this because we knew we needed a break, and we also knew keeping our marriage alive was "priceless." I am confident dating frequently is less expensive than divorce in the long run. So, continual courtship is totally worth it!

Another key ingredient to keeping your health and sanity during times of great stress: knowing your spouse has your back when you have a bad day. You can tag them and take a break for a while.

Tamara's Journal, August 14, 2001

I had a hard day today with the kids—just trying to haul them around and do stuff is hard! I was bawling by the time Justin came home. Nathan hadn't napped and was super-cranky!

Justin told me to take off and get a break. I went out by myself and finished buying material for the curtains in the kitchen area.

Tamara's Journal, September 1, 2001

It was a long day! I was up and got ready early. Nathan was good until about 8:00 am, then he started being grouchy. The kids wore me out today! I was so exhausted—not enough mama breaks! I am glad to have a husband who comes home and helps me.

Having a partner, friend, companion, or spouse that can pitch hit and give you some time off is essential. Most books and advice on surviving difficult times strongly recommend this. If you don't have someone already able to step in and fill this role, take steps to find something that works for you.

Not everyone has a spouse, and sometimes family is far away or may not be the most supportive. You might have to get creative and explore other avenues. Church groups might be a possibility, or support groups that specifically focus on your particular battle (there are support groups for just about every imaginable struggle or diagnosis). Don't hesitate to initiate contact with one of these if spouse, friends, or family are not an ideal option for you.

On a side note, you might also explore things you can do solo to save your sanity: watch a funny show, read, go out on the back deck and watch clouds or stars for five minutes (assuming you've locked the kids in a safe place).

One way or another, you have to have some support, or your mental, emotional, and physical health will suffer. It's the old idea of putting your oxygen mask on before you save others. If you don't help yourself, you can't help anyone else.

Teachers & Therapists

God blessed us with mostly phenomenal teachers through my children's schooling. From preschool to elementary school, we had such amazing and supportive teachers. Jacob and Nathan both started kindergarten in an autism classroom in our school district. Nathan spent most of his time in the autism classroom getting therapy specific to him along with speech therapy, occupational therapy, and physical therapy.

When Jacob started kindergarten, I was so worried—first because he was so busy, and secondly because he turned five in mid-August and was a young kindergartener. His first year he spent 90% of the time in the autism room and 10% in his regular kindergarten classroom. His Special Ed teacher held him back and he repeated kindergarten. That second year, he learned more social skills and by the end spent 70% of his time in regular kindergarten class and 30% in the autism classroom. Baby steps.

Jacob and Nathan's elementary school head autism teacher, Mrs. B., and her aides were our godsend. There was so much we were still learning, and she taught us little tricks and tips. I remember going to observe her classroom one day before summer break so I could learn the "morning routine" at school and implement it at home during the summer break. I learned so much about maintaining a routine from her and having a visual schedule. Mrs. B. also taught us many occupational therapy skills I could work on at home.

Mrs. B's classroom was an amazing wonderland for children on the spectrum to touch and feel sensory items, follow along with books on tape, do puzzles, jump, run and spin, use weighted vests, and progress educationally. One great skill she taught Nathan was how to do "touch math." It was an amazing method which taught him how to add. She was knowledgeable and helpful, creative and kind, patient and wonderful.

This woman was one of my support saviors in the early years of diagnosis. If I had a dilemma, she was one of the people I would go to and ask. She had decades of experience, whereas I was a newbie. I love her and keep in touch with her to this day.

JUSTIN: Many times it wasn't luck or chance in the teachers assigned to our special needs children. Tamara worked closely with the Special Ed team to get them assigned to teachers who had that extra special ability to help our child.

We also learned so many tips and tricks from therapists along the way—from pre-school clear through to high school. God bless the therapists out there! They taught me so many things I could carry over from the educational setting to the home setting.

I am also thankful I usually felt I was a part of a team when I went to IEP meetings (Individualized Education Program—the document the schools use to help children with unique needs progress). Granted, I have had some instances where I have had to fight for my kids and their continued services. I am sure every parent with a child in Special Ed has had to do this at least once. However, for the most part we have been blessed to have wonderful resources in teachers and therapists.

Support Groups

When you are dealing with any type of diagnosis, it is typical to seek out others in a similar situation. We joined the autism support group in our local area and they were a huge support. I loved how they offered friendship, information, and a group of others we could bond with and share suggestions and ask questions. Joining a support group is always a great approach when facing diagnosis.

With the expansion of the internet, this has become

even easier because people can find support groups online—without even leaving the confines of their own home. What a tremendous resource for someone who is in "survival mode" to know they are not alone. I wish we would have had more online resources when I was raising my kids.

The support group also kept us informed of conferences or classes we could take. We took advantage of these (adding tools to our toolbox of learning) and mingling with them continued to expand our network of families affected by the same diagnosis.

Doctors and Health Care Providers

Having a good doctor and other health care providers to guide you through any diagnosis is vital. It is important to find someone you can trust, someone who can explain things in lay-man's terms, and someone who you feel comfortable with.

I am so thankful for dedicated health care professionals. They have helped us through some bumps like helping us know what to do to help Nathan sleep better. When Justin and I finally took Nathan to a neurologist in 2009 in desperation after not sleeping well for many years, I am sure the doctor took one look at the bags under our eyes and took pity on us.

We explained Nathan needed a solution that didn't require swallowing pills. It had to be chewable. He suggested melatonin (before it became wildly popular). Just saying this word makes me smile: Melatonin. I swear it saved my life—maybe my son's life too. This was our neurologist's suggestion. Melatonin is a natural hormone made by your pineal gland that helps control your sleep cycle. It is awesome they make chewable supplements of it—this is perfect for my boys.

Oh, the difference it has made! Instead of lying in bed for three to four hours wide awake at bedtime, Nathan was asleep within thirty to sixty minutes of us giving him the melatonin. Can I get a "Hallelujah?" Thank you, dear doctor, for saving our sleep!

> **JUSTIN:** The doctor who helped us was so amazing! He found the formula that would work for Nathan, and probably added ten years to my and Tamara's lives—now that we are getting semi-regular sleep!

Doctors have been at our side during every diagnosis. I am thankful for their kind words, their patience with me as I muddled through such a steep learning curve, and their guidance when we needed help with diets, allergic reactions, sensitivities, bowel issues and exhaustion.

Find a good doctor and cling to them during any diagnosis and treatment. Health care professionals can also help with extended treatment. Be sure to find a good nurse or therapist that truly cares or feels it is their calling in life to lift and serve. Some professionals seem to rush in and out without much more than "Hello," and "Here is your prescription." Asking around in support groups will give you a good start on who others have found to be helpful with your diagnosis.

Also, realize there are true experts out there in your field of diagnosis. Seek them out. The quality of care you will receive will be night and day.

Extended Family

Family can be a great support or a curse during any diagnosis. We won the family lottery because we were blessed with supportive family on both sides. Parents and siblings have loved us and helped us and supported us through all our autism-related challenges. They were always a listening ear when we needed to talk, vent, or ask for help.

Unfortunately, we have never lived close to family, so this has been a more difficult resource to tap into. During our "survival years" we had once-a-year visits out west to visit for family reunions. And of course, those changes in our schedule were always difficult for our boys on the spectrum.

We were blessed to have several family members come and watch our kids once a year during a little get-away Justin and I started doing around the same time as our ten-year-anniversary. We would carefully write out the "Anderson Family Bible" as a resource to whomever was brave enough to watch our kids and off we went. What great family members we have!

> **JUSTIN:** Calling our siblings or parents by the title of "angel" would be an understatement! I'm sure they were less than happy to relieve us for a spell, but they never showed it. They even laughed when they told us how Jacob, then an energetic two-year-old, pulled the fire alarm at church, interrupting the main service for the next hour while the local leaders tried to figure out how to reset the alarm box!

We are so thankful for the wonderful extended family we have and wish we lived closer to them. I am thankful they have been a support to us and love us and our children just as we are.

Friends

When you live far from family, friends become a key "support group." I was blessed to find many friends at church and in our neighborhood.

One of the women who became my dear friends was our realtor, Carolyn Vernetti. She not only helped us find our house, but kept in touch as we acclimatized to living in Arkansas. Shortly after Nathan was diagnosed and Justin and I were in "denial," I received an unexpected phone call from Carolyn wondering if I could do lunch with her sometime.

I arranged for Justin to watch the kids one day while I went to lunch with Carolyn. This was how our conversation played out:

"How are you?"

I answered, "Fine."

"No, really. How are you doing?"

The dam burst! I remember tearfully sharing with her about Nathan's diagnosis. This was something I hadn't even shared with other close friends. She listened with compassion as I explained how lost I felt learning about autism and how I didn't know where to even begin.

Then she made a suggestion I truly appreciated. Carolyn had struggled with diabetes for years and said the thing that helped her as she was learning about diabetes was making a binder with all the tests performed on her, doctors notes, suggestions, ideas, etc. I took this advice to heart! I made a binder where I kept Nathan's diagnosis papers, therapies we tried, information on different diets, etc. It helped me have one place where I could keep track of everything.

To this day, I am grateful Carolyn followed her impression to call me up and ask me to go to lunch. She was God's angel to me. I am also thankful she suggested making a binder with information and notes. It helped me in the early days of diagnosis.

This is the value of dear friends! Even when they don't struggle with the same diagnosis, they can be a listening ear when the burden seems too heavy to carry on your own. My life has been blessed by dear friends who were God's angels to me in times of heartache and trial.

Extra Help/Respite

We have the honor of having an "adopted" sibling. Her name is Melissa, and she was my angel. The summer I was pregnant with Noelle I quickly found I could not physically even keep up with my kids, especially Jacob, who was constantly trying to escape. So, after much prayer we decided to hire one of the young girls from church that babysat for our family to come and help work alongside me as a nanny. This is Melissa.

Tamara's Journal, July 21, 2004

Melissa helped me take the kids swimming this afternoon and that was actually pretty fun. I think we all had a good time.

Tamara's Newsletter to family, April 5, 2007

> We have also been blessed to have the help of a wonderful college-age young lady, Melissa, who helps Tamara with the boys and all of her crazy-insane projects. There is no way I could do much of this without her help. It is especially nice to have her around when Justin is traveling, and when we decide to go on field trips with all the kids during the summer. With both Jacob and Nathan being autistic there is no way I could go anywhere without help.

She ended up being our nanny all through her high school years and some summers of her college years. Even with the two of us watching the four kids, Jacob would sometimes escape our home and yard. She was the one I depended on to help me in my quest to keep active and do excursions in the community.

I just didn't have enough hands to keep hold of my three youngest when Justin was at work. So she came daily Monday through Friday in the summers to help me keep a schedule for my autistic boys, and keep them safe and accounted for when we went to visit pet stores, parks, libraries, and museums. I think I would have holed up and died if not for Melissa.

In summary, it is vital to build a network of friends, family, doctors, therapists, teachers and supporters to cheer you on once a loved one has been diagnosed with something life-changing. I have discovered it isn't a weakness to build lasting friendships—it is a strength. These people are your angels. Pray to find them, and don't be afraid to ask for help when you need it. It helps to know you are not alone!

One more suggestion that can help during diagnosis: help others. This can seem counter-intuitive, but it helps on so many levels—even if it's just to get your mind off your own worries. Helping someone else with their struggles gives an added perspective on your own sorrows. This can even happen in an online support group. You can reap blessings by helping others. I don't know how or why it works, only that I have seen my burdens lift when I have reached out to serve—even amid my own grief.

PEACE AND ACCEPTANCE AT LAST

THROUGH THE YEARS OF post-diagnosis struggle, I wish I could say there was some magic wand I waved and everything was great—I was happy and at peace. But it was hard work. The journey to peace was fraught with uphill battles and tumbles down steep mountain slopes. I can finally look back and say there were a few key things which helped me come to terms with God.

I also want to clarify that these are things that helped me on *my journey.* I encourage you to be prayerful and incorporate what you feel are the best things to help you on *your journey*—because we are on different paths.

1. I went to church WEEKLY.

This was so, so difficult. Jacob was constantly trying

to escape the pew. My husband and I had to have lightning-fast reflexes to keep him with us. We were loud and it was hard to keep the kids quiet. It must have been difficult for those around us to concentrate on the meeting. Nevertheless, I was blessed by kind souls in our congregation who were thoughtful and sweet and oh so understanding as week after week we kept coming back.

Tamara's Journal, May 18, 2003

It was a hard day at church with Nathan. He screamed and cried through most of the meeting. Justin and I were both moved to tears. It is *so* hard.

Justin and I sang in an octet, "Lord, I Would Follow Thee," and I had to try not to think too hard about the words so I could stay composed during the song. What poignant words we had to sing, "In the quiet heart is hidden sorrow that the eye can't see . . . Find in thee my strength, my beacon."

I feel so weak, so overwhelmed. I feel like I don't know how to approach this. I want to have hope, but I feel like my burden is heavy today.

I vividly remember another particularly difficult Sunday. The kids had been awful. We arrived later than usual to church and the spot where we usually sat was occupied—so we had to sit in the back. The change in seating triggered my kids to behave more terribly than usual. I could barely keep them quiet, and I couldn't hear the speaker. I pulled every toy out of my bag trying to keep the kids happy and somewhat quiet. But by the end of the meeting every toy and book and puzzle was flung all over the row—cars and trains, books and Cheerios lay under every chair. I felt drained. Justin took the kids off to their classes, and I exhaustedly tackled the mess we had created.

While I was cleaning up our disaster, a dear older man came up to me and said, "Sister Anderson, how are you doing?" I broke down in tears. (I am sure this is not the response he was expecting.) He came over and gave me a hug, reassuring me it would be okay and things would get easier. I thank God for sweet people like this who were kind as we struggled to come.

> **JUSTIN:** We have some good friends, the Conover family, who went to church with us when we lived in Arkansas. Their family moved away for a few months and they sent us an email saying their kids were now the loudest in their church. After one meeting, they said to each other, "We sure miss the Anderson's." I guess our family was so loud, energetic, and disruptive, that it made the other families feel good about themselves!

Then there were the Sunday school teachers which were assigned to our kids. They always had at least two in my autistic kids' classrooms (and one of them was watching/caring for my sons full-time.) Inevitably these teachers learned to love my sweet kids—energy, autism, and all. And I loved them for loving my kids (and giving me a break to feed my soul).

One story is funny to look back on now, although it was awful when it happened. It occurred when Jacob was three or four. I was enjoying a Sunday School lesson, happy for a moment of peace, when one of Jacob's teachers walked in the room with a panicked look on her face. I immediately followed her out into the hall where she explained Jacob had gotten away from her and had run into the other congregation's meeting. Oh snap!

I peeked into their meeting and lo and behold, there was my Jacob up in front of the entire congregation, running back and forth behind the speaker, giggling gleefully. *Great! Now we not only are disrupting our meetings, but others' meetings as well.*

Steeling myself, I walked to the front of their congregation and chased my son back and forth for a minute before some considerate soul helped me corner him. Then I threw Jacob over my shoulder and headed for the exit just as fast as I could while I turned fifty shades of red.

Embarrassed? Absolutely! *This is my life. What the heck?*

After Sundays like this, you better believe there were weeks I did not want to go to church. It would have been so much easier to just stay home. But I thought to myself, *What example do I want to set for my kids? Do I want to teach them God is important to me, even and especially when it is hard? YES!* So, I kept going. It is a good thing I am so stubborn.

Since children with autism thrive on patterns and schedules I *knew* if I could just get this pattern and schedule of weekly church established in their lives when they were little, it would be worth it, right? Oh, how I hoped it would be worth it—because I was working so hard at keeping them quiet. And I was having a hard time hearing the message—and I needed that message of peace in my life right then. My soul felt parched, hungry, and starved for peace.

Persistence did pay off. Unbelievably, we can now sit on the front pew of the church without anyone escaping. I never thought the day would come! We can sit without making much disruption or without bringing a diaper bag brimming with toys. Nathan has a little roller bag with his stickers which keep him occupied and mostly quiet—although hc has still been known to bellow out "Oh! Susanna, oh don't you cry for me" in the middle of church.

One friend recently told me, "I love sitting by you guys and listening to him sing. It makes the church meeting much more fun!"

2. I read the scriptures and prayed DAILY.

My day was filled from sun-up to sun-down, so sometimes it was only a verse or two per day and a quick muttered prayer before I fell into bed. But other times I could fit in a whole chapter or a lengthy prayer. My soul needed nourishment because emotionally, I was a wreck, and I knew I needed to gain a greater and truer trust in God.

Tamara's Journal, February 6, 2003

I have made a commitment to myself to study/read my scriptures daily before I read my comics section of the newspaper. I have started a study of a cool topic and I feel so renewed! I feel like my spirit inside my body is teaching my physical mind things I once knew and understood.

> Today I read Romans 8:5–17 and for the first time I understood something.
>
> "For they that are after the flesh do mind the things of the flesh; but they that are after the Spirit the things of the Spirit...For as many as are led by the Spirit of God, they are the sons [and daughters] of God."
>
> This is what I wrote: "Impatience is a mortal trait. Our spirit, or who we truly are, is a patient person. Therefore, we need to strengthen our spirit and subdue our mortal body to be subject to who we really are. This is the meaning of being 'true to ourselves,' true to our eternal self."

I needed to be more like Shadrach, Meshach, and Abed-nego. Would I ever reach that level of faith? Would I ever give it to God and say, "Thy will be done?"

Reading their story and other stories in the scriptures helped teach me I wasn't the only one with problems. Think of Joseph in Egypt. Man! If anyone had reason to complain, it was him. Things seemed to go from bad to worse with Joseph. Sold by his brothers to the Ishmaelites, ending up a slave in Egypt, and then thrown in prison after being falsely accused. How could it get much worse? But then God opened a door for him, which led him to Pharaoh's court where God used him to save not only Egypt but his father's family as well.

Stories like this gave me hope and faith that though my life seemed pretty bad, at least I wasn't in jail or hadn't been falsely accused. At least I had family members who loved me. These scripture stories gave me hope something good would come from it. And so, I kept reading my scriptures and looking for examples of hope and faith to boost me along.

One of my favorite verses in the New Testament is found in Matthew 11:28-30, "Come unto me, all ye that labour and are heavy laden, and I will give you rest. *Take my yoke upon you, and learn of me* . . . and ye shall find rest unto your souls. For my yoke is easy and my burden is light."

I love the image of a yoke. It was used in the olden days to hook two oxen or horses together so they could work together to pull a heavy load. I have learned through the years I had to choose to yoke myself to an all-powerful God to pull my heavy load. To have God take my burdens, I needed to be willing to get to know Him and learn of him. I did this through simple things like reading the scriptures, praying, and going to church. As I prioritized and did these simple things first, I found I did feel yoked to God, and even though I spent additional time praying and reading each day, the benefit of having God help me with my burden was worth the effort.

Being a mother to young children is exhausting, even under the best of circumstances. I read journal entry after journal entry of early wakings, chasing children all day, dealing with so many colds, flu bugs, and bouts of bronchitis, diarrhea, teething, and finally collapsing in bed each night. I was so exhausted *All. The. Time!*

I needed God's help simply to survive daily—especially dealing with the emotions of coming to terms with autism. So, regular scripture study coupled with prayer was my spiritual food I needed just as much as I craved physical food.

I prayed and asked God if I put in my little bit of effort to read the scriptures if He would bless me and help me to gain understanding and faith. I prayed I could learn from these examples of great scriptural people. God blessed me. I survived. Some days I survived just barely, but I leaned on God and strove to strengthen my faith.

JUSTIN: We have also held family scripture study daily for most of our married lives. This has benefited us, and me, so much over the years. Our early days of scripture study involved a picture version with very basic language so little children could understand. As the children matured, we moved to the regular scriptures. Each child would read a verse or two, and then we would discuss what we had learned. Those that couldn't read were asked to repeat what we said.

I feel this has blessed us in many ways. We discuss the nature of God. Who is he? What does he do? What does he want? How do we talk to him? It is fun to discuss the stories and experiences told in the scriptures. We also discuss how to apply the gospel in our lives. We encourage our children to ask questions, or we ask them questions. By starting this early in life, we have seen changes in the quality and quantity of our study as our children get older.

Tamara's Journal, April 26, 2001

Even though Justin left today on a business trip, I feel like I have been blessed so much and at peace. What great blessings from God! I have noticed on the days when I read my scriptures and pray, He blesses me!

One Sunday I wrote in my journal about stories recounted in Hebrews 11 of the many things people accomplished by faith.

"By faith Noah, being warned of God of things not seen as yet, moved with fear, prepared an ark to the saving of his house . . . and became heir of the righteousness which is by faith . . .

Through faith also Sara herself received strength to conceive seed, and was delivered of a child when she was past age, because she judged him faithful who had promised . . .

By faith Abraham, when he was tried, offered up Isaac . . . accounting that God was able to raise him up, even from the dead . . .

By faith Moses . . . refused to be called the son of Pharaoh's daughter; choosing rather to suffer affliction with the people of God . . . by faith he forsook Egypt . . . [and] passed through the Red sea as by dry land."[27]

Yes, it took great faith for people to do hard things in the scriptures. Some of them were "saved" or had miracles happen after wading through trials, while others were "stoned, sawn asunder, tempted [and]

27 Hebrews 11:7, 11, 17-19, 24, 25, 27, 29

slain by the sword."[28] In other words, I learned that having faith my kids would be healed didn't necessarily guarantee great and mighty miracles would happen. I wrote in my journal that evening,

"Great challenges make great men and women."

I learned by studying my scriptures I wanted to be a great woman who had faith during all seasons of my life.

I wanted to add my own verse to Hebrews 11 about Tamara. If I did, it would have gone something like this:

By faith Tamara, when she had difficult obstacles, endured hardship for a season; trusting God would be faithful and strengthen her to raise a righteous family.

I know it may sound ridiculous to put write myself a "verse," but I tried to have the scriptures come alive for me. I tried to walk in their shoes—because I knew if they could go through hard things and stay faithful to God, I could too. And I clung to that!

And God did help me and save me day after day, early morning after late night. I fought and clung to God because I knew no one else knew my pain and my sorrow and my grief. I knew no one else knew my heartache, my desires, and my weaknesses. I felt like scripture study and prayer bound me to God when I had no one else to grasp on to.

3. I developed my creative talents and found stress relief.

I think this is especially important for stay-at-home moms or any caregiver who is working all day to help and care

---

28 Hebrews 11:37

for others. It would have been so easy for me to be self-absorbed and isolate myself from everyone, but I think I would have only felt more alone if I had done that.

Staying involved was made easier by the fact I had a supportive husband. He would come home from work and happily give me a break (so I didn't go completely insane).

What did I do outside of my home? I was involved in the youth program at my church. I loved those teens and felt a kinship to so many of them—because I too felt a bit like a teenager at times—lost and drifting and unsure about the strength of my faith. I also had learned a few things about loving and trusting God, and somehow teaching others about this, helped me be more sure of it myself.

Tamara's Journal, October 14, 2004

The young women did some displays tonight of the projects they have been working on. One of the girls did her genealogy and started her personal history. She thanked one of the other leaders and I for getting her started. How exciting it has been for her. Sometimes it is nice to know you are making a difference.

Tamara's Journal, October 27, 2004

I had a great time with the young women tonight! We made Halloween cookies and decorated them. One of the girls came and told me she wanted to learn the gospel again if I was willing to teach her. I told her I'd be happy to. I hope she comes. I know God wants her to learn.

I also was involved in organizing a regional choral Christmas Concert. This was a challenge and a blessing. It was a challenge because it was hard and required significant work to pull off yearly. But it was a blessing to me because it made me think about something other than myself and my children with autism. And I needed a break from my kids occasionally.

I needed time where I was working on developing my talents outside of motherhood—time where I was developing who Tamara was and what her gifts were other than struggling to parent some challenging children.

> **JUSTIN:** I had a very different way to release my stress. Going to work got me away from the hourly challenges Tamara faced. So, the stresses of home were separate from the challenges at work.
>
> It took me a while to branch out and do some things I enjoyed. I started to take my oldest son golfing. I don't have the patience to do 18 holes, so we'd find a pitch and putt a 9-hole course. I also joined a racquet club and played racquetball with a friend and co-worker. Plus, our office got a ping pong table to help us release some steam and I got pretty good at that too. I also enjoy going to a football or basketball game with friends or our children. I was also involved in Cub and Boy Scouts as a leader while working with my sons.
>
> I'm a big fan of the late Stephen Covey and his book *Seven Habits of Highly Effective People*. One key principle he teaches is that we all need to relax and refresh ourselves. He calls it "loosening

the bow" which means finding ways to not be so tightly strung in life.

I remember a co-worker who was so determined to reach his work goals that he refused to take vacation until he did. Finally, after much pleading, he paused and took a few days off. He came back a very happy person and found a renewed energy in his job. Please, find something to rejuvenate your soul and make it a priority in your life.

Developing talents is important whether you are struggling with children on the autism spectrum, health challenges or life in general. Put social media away for a few hours and take time to invest in yourself. Maybe you will like painting or writing or playing an instrument. You are never too old to learn new things. This truly can be such a blessing. As you are successful, you will inevitably find that your confidence grows in your new-found abilities. This confidence will spill over and help in other areas in your life where you are struggling.

Tamara's Journal, December 14, 2003

Yesterday and today were the two performances of the Chorale. The Interfaith performance Saturday night was miraculous because the Lord tempered the weather so we could have the performance. It snowed three inches or more and yet the streets didn't collect snow. They were totally dry as I drove home. It was fun to have other choirs perform along with us. Our choir did a great job.

Tonight's performance was wonderful and well-attended. It has been thrilling to conduct such a large choir. The spirit was there as we sang of our dear Savior and hearts were touched. So many people commented how much they loved it and asked when we could do it again.

A friend commented last night "this is the thing you were born to do." It is! I have loved it! I am so grateful the Lord has enabled me to develop these talents. It has been so fun!

Tamara's Journal, December 5, 2004

It was an amazing and hectic day! Justin left on a trip today, so I was solo with the four kids during church. It was crazy! The Lord did send people to help me though. One friend moved to the pew right behind us because Jacob kept escaping between the end of the pew and the wall to the bench behind us. She also helped with the kids during our huge dress rehearsal for choir.

Another woman just sat and cuddled Noelle the whole time—so sweet! So in spite of us being at church for six hours, we did survive. The Chorale sounded wonderful! They are going to do a great job.

One of the youth leaders gave a great lesson to the young women today about talents. It truly made me think about some talents the Lord has given me—particularly in music. The hard thing about getting a talent from God is He expects us to develop it and work at it and use it—not hide it. It isn't easy and requires significant time, effort, and sacrifice.

While she was speaking I got this idea about the next "project" God wants me to tackle. There is this awesome play/cantata I think God wants us to do. As I thought about this I wondered, *Dear God, Why do they always have to be such* huge *ordeals?* The answer came back as a whisper in my mind, *Why do you think I have blessed you with these talents?*

Sometimes I wonder why God has blessed me with such "obvious" talents (ones which are noticeable) vs. service or patience—I'd like those. I don't know the answer to this dilemma. Even though the tasks seem daunting (I'm overwhelmed thinking about them) I know God will open a path so I can accomplish these things.

I found great fulfillment and joy in serving and developing my talents. Music is also healing—and the power of listening to and helping others perform such beautiful Christmas music soothed my troubled soul and fueled my faith in Christ. I was so thankful for this blessing in my life.

Make a list of things you would like to learn or do, and then make it happen. You too can find a "release" and confidence by developing new talents. This will give you a break from the wearing of daily routines and help you keep perspective as you "get away" for a few moments from caregiving.

It is also imperative to find other stress-relievers. Some ideas that I have implemented or seen others use with success are: meditating, deep breathing, massage, yoga, laughing, exercising, reading a good book, watching happy movies, napping, journaling, and taking a walk, hike, or drive. If you are experiencing high amounts of stress, find a release. Everything seems better when you take a little time to relax, relieve stress, and find joy outside of "diagnosis."

4. I counted and recorded my blessings!

When life is difficult it is so easy to find the negative things in life and be completely overwhelmed by them. I was so thankful I kept a journal of those early years when things were so tough. I think by journaling on a regular daily basis, I processed the hard events and annotated the blessings.

Don't misunderstand—I wrote about bad days and things as well as the good. But I think it was an important step for me to learn to look for good things even in trying circumstances.

Studies have been done on the benefits of gratitude. Being grateful 1) Improves physical and psychological health, 2) Improves sleep, 3) Increases self-esteem and mental strength, and 4) Opens the door to more friendships. These are incredible benefits from gratitude.

Tamara's Journal, April 27, 2001

This week is practically over. I am relieved we have gotten so much done with regards to our move. I feel God has again blessed me to be busy and get stuff done. A friend came over and helped me with a project today. That was a fun break from all the phone calls and stress of the move. She is truly wonderful!

I love my sons too. They are so sweet! They are my real treasures. I love Nathan's chubby little hands and sweet smile. I love the way Jordan's eyes twinkle with excitement when he is happy. I love hearing Nathan sing, "I am a Child of God" on his own. I love hearing Jordan tell me "the sun is up" when it comes out from behind the clouds. I miss my husband (he's on another business trip), but my soul is full of joy for the many blessings I do have.

Tamara"s Journal, February 15, 2003

Well, these last few days haven't exactly turned out how I would have liked. Justin had a sinus infection and now he has strep throat on top of it. Poor guy! I had to take him to the emergency room today because he was running a fever and he was on an antibiotic and getting worse.

We weren't able to go to the Winter Ball tonight, and I have been a little bummed, but I can't help but chuckle at our luck in February. Two years ago, we were in the car accident, last year Nathan broke his arm, and this year Justin is in the hospital. It must be our hospital month.

Looking back, I am so grateful for the opportunity to be alive. I still have problems with my rib, back and collarbone, but I have been blessed. I am grateful for the wonderful friends we have made here in Arkansas. We have been blessed to have another sweet little boy, Nathan is improving, I have a sweet and wonderful husband and great extended family. Oh yes, God has blessed me so much! I feel I will be forever in His debt.

Tamara's Journal, December 5, 2004

I had a sweet thing happen with Nathan tonight. After he said his prayers and climbed into bed I told him "I love you, Nathan." He then wrapped his arm around my neck and held me cheek to cheek for 30 seconds.

Now, this may not seem like a huge deal, but it was one of the first times he has ever initiated a hug where *he* actually did the hugging. Usually it is us hugging him and him sitting there with limp arms. The Lord truly is great and merciful! I am so grateful!

I have a dear friend named Suzanne. She is the mother of three children with dietary issues and severe food allergies. One of her children even had to have a pump put into her stomach to feed her because her food allergies were so severe, she wasn't gaining weight.

Through the process of trying one food at a time, they are figuring out which foods she can tolerate, and which she can't. Suzanne has learned the science of cooking so she can make meals her children can eat. She has been through a lot and could have easily taken a negative outlook on life. Instead, she is one of the most positive people I have ever met!

Suzanne was in a car accident a few years ago which left her with a broken rib and bruised shins (among other things). Her doctor told her to take it easy for a while. When I went to visit her, she shared with me a new perspective on an old cliché. The saying goes, "When life hands you lemons, make lemonade!" Suzanne then commented you can't make lemonade out of just lemons. You need to find something sugary to sweeten it with, or you are going to have some very tart lemonade.

Suzanne had been trying to take it easy after the accident, and she allowed people to come in and serve her. She told me she had figured out in difficult situations it is best to look for little moments of sweetness God sends along the way. As she looked for them, she found them: a child's embrace, a friend's visit, a meal delivered, or a kitchen swept. All these things helped her sweeten her tart lemons into lemonade!

Suzanne could have easily looked at her situation and bemoaned how unfair it all was. But God taught her if you approach life with love and a grateful heart, you will find sweet moments which make even the hardest of journeys a little better.

I learned, just as Suzanne did, even amid the worst times of our life, we can look for little miracles, little gems of "sweetness" to help us survive. Count those blessings! Write them down. Along the toughest detoured roads of life, make time to pause, smell the roses along the path beside you, reflect on your gratitude for the things you have instead of the things you don't and the journey will not be so weighty. Look for and celebrate moments of joy!

JUSTIN: One time we decided to have the entire family make a list of things we are grateful for. We placed paper on the table and let the kids write anything that came to them: Video games, friends, air, mom's cooking, electricity, etc.

Then we took those papers and taped them together, making a long nine-foot roll of paper. I got out a ladder and taped that list to the wall near the top of the ceiling and we left the list there for a couple of months. This became a great reminder of the blessings and benefits we experience all the time.

Peace—Finally!

These are the things which helped me finally come around to acceptance: Going to church, praying and reading my scriptures, serving and developing my talents, and counting my blessings. It was a continual cycle of reliance of God, finally brought me around to peace.

Your journey to peace may look similar to mine, or may look totally different than mine—and that is okay. We are each on our "normal for me" paths.

I finally came to feel a peace with my children being on the autism spectrum. It didn't come as fast as I would have liked, but it finally came.

Tamara's Journal, August 06, 2006

My soul hungered tonight. I felt the need to talk to my Heavenly Father. What a blessing it is to pray—to have our prayers reach high to the heavens and to have a loving Father come and listen.

I am amazed as I look back over the past year—what a difference! Last year at this point I was struggling through a difficult summer with Nathan. I was dealing with challenging emotions that Jacob was autistic. I couldn't put him in a normal preschool. I was angry, frustrated, overwhelmed, and exhausted. Even though I knew I shouldn't ask, *Why me,* it had passed through my mind. *Don't I already have enough I am dealing with?*

Now, there is a peace. There was a talk a few years ago entitled, "But if not." It was a powerful talk which spoke to my soul. I always wondered if I would have the faith to say, "I know you have the power to heal my sons, but if not I will be just fine." I finally reached that point tonight, and I am amazed. There has been much healing which has taken place in my soul over the past year. My burdens have been lifted, and through the Savior's infinite tender mercies, He has strengthened me so I could bear the burdens placed upon my back—even so much that I feel like I can submit cheerfully to God's will.

I know in His strength I can do all things (Philippians 4:3). I don't know if it is my lot in life to ever be freed from the challenge and blessing of having children with special needs, but I am grateful for them and what the Lord has taught me because of them.

We have had such a wonderful summer full of fun and adventures. I am almost sad this year to see them go back to school. I never thought I would say that either. It just goes to show the Lord truly can change our hearts and mine is becoming more of a "mother-heart." (I was a little rough around the edges before and I still have a long way to go, but with the Lord's help I know I will get there someday.)

I'm sure this is what God saw in me all along. I know I didn't walk this path alone. The peace of acceptance had not come easily, but I could now say just like Shadrach, Meshach, and Abed-nego, I had come to know and trust God more in my times of trial. I had also learned He didn't leave me alone in my fiery furnace. He came to me and strengthened me and helped me along until I was strong enough to walk on my own.

I could now say, "I know God can heal my boys, *but if not,* I still believe He will provide a way for my family to find joy." I was finally able to change my expectations to include His . . . a more eternal perspective.

What an uphill journey toward final peace and acceptance. I am so thankful that I was stubborn enough to keep going to church and put myself in a place where I was spiritually fed. I was also so thankful for scripture study and daily prayer. What a privilege it was to get out and serve others in my community and develop my talents and record my blessings along the way. These four things helped me finally progress toward inner peace and greater faith that everything would indeed turn out okay in the end.

THE JOURNEY

Successful Baby Steps

A FEW YEARS AGO, after our family had moved to Spring, Texas, we decided to take a walk around our small neighborhood to see the new construction. We took our entire family with us and had an iPod on hand in case Nathan (then twelve years old) decided he wasn't going to walk with us. Believe it or not, we made it around the block and nobody had a tantrum, or needed the iPod as a distracter.

As we came around the final bend to see our home my husband commented, "We just took a family walk." The profoundness of what he said shocked me! My mind reeled back to the spring evening years before in Arkansas which started this journey of me redefining what "normal" was for my family. Wow! We had done it. We took a family walk! The walk didn't last more than five minutes, but we had actually done it! I doubt anyone who didn't know my family intimately would have understood the immensity of that accomplishment. It was awesome!

Not to be outdone by the walk, I decided we should do a family bike ride. My husband even thought I was crazy. Every time we had tried to go on a family bike ride, Nathan wouldn't leave our little subdivision. So, I decided to think "outside the box" on this one.

One evening, we loaded all the bikes in the back of the pickup truck and drove about a mile away. We parked the pickup truck and unloaded the bikes. Then we told the kids we would ride home on our bikes. Nathan particularly wasn't happy with me, but he got on his four-wheel pedal bike and away we went. There were a few stops along the way home, helping kids with this or that, but we eventually got back into our subdivision. Just as we turned the corner onto our street, Jacob's pant leg got caught in his bike, and he wiped out. I carefully untangled him from his bike, wiped his tears (partly from crashing and partly from not being the first one home), and we made it home. We took pictures of another monumental achievement for our family!

Our triumphs might seem simple or crazy to some people, but they are amazingly huge for our "normal" little family. After moving to Utah, we had another huge accomplishment: We hiked up to Delicate Arch in Arches National Park with our *entire family!* For those of you who haven't done this hike, it is about a three-mile hike which gains about 480 feet in altitude.

There is even a part of the trail which has a sheer drop-off on one side (just enough to make my stomach drop). I repeatedly told the kids to hug the mountain and stay away from the edge. I also kept Nathan by my side. He did much of the hike with an iPod in his hand, but he came happily! Believe me, my husband and I both prayed and asked God to help Nathan make it because we all wanted to go see this amazing wonder of nature. I can still hardly believe we made it. God is indeed a God of miracles!

JUSTIN: That was an epic hike for our family and Nathan. It went well beyond a stroll around the block, so to do a difficult hike for many miles with elevation change was nothing short of a miracle! This was one of those days where I felt overwhelmed with gratitude and joy.

Now Nathan has an Access Pass (or Disability pass) to visit any National Park in the United States. And we use it! He's done hikes in Zion, Bryce Canyon, Arches, Canyonlands, Capitol Reef, Yellowstone, Mesa Verde and the Grand Canyon. Mesa Verde was such a kick! This is one of the original parks created by Theodore Roosevelt and it protects the cliff dwellings for the indigenous people from 700 years ago. They have special hikes you can book with park rangers where you visit some of these amazing cliff dwellings up close. I emphasize "cliff" here because you have to hike very narrow, steep trails, climb large wooden ladders over 20 feet high, squeeze into small tunnels less than 18 inches wide, and climb steep ledges with chains for a guide rail. Yet Nathan made it through all these obstacles with very little concern or resistance from him.

Can you believe it? This is the same family who didn't make it 200 feet from our house before he blew up in fits and tantrums. This has been a testament to patience, perseverance, faith, endurance, prayers, blessings, and hope. My hope for anyone still reading this book is that you conquer your life's challenges and find what is normal for you, through God's help.

I have had people ask me what am I going to do when my children with special needs reach a certain age. The thought perplexes me at times and overwhelms me as well. So, I have decided to prepare for the future but not try to figure it out right now. I have learned God has guided me on my journey bit-by-bit. So, bit-by-bit, and problem-by-problem I will take my cares to Him and trust He will lead me to the right path for our "normal" family. We have moved several times, and though challenging, God has opened doors for us at each place we have lived. I have learned to trust Him more perfectly.

You, too, can find peace along your "normal for you" journey no matter what life detours you may face. I hope you have found a few ideas or principles among my musings that you feel you can apply to your life. God can help you find things that work perfectly for you and your situation as you learn to develop true faith, lean on Him when things get too hard to handle, and find value in who you really are as a child of God.

Peace is a journey of baby steps and sometimes looks like two steps forward and one step back. But keep moving, keep going forward. Don't compare yourself to others! You are on your own journey. Learn tricks of the trade and put them in your toolbox of learning, and find your support group to guide you through life's storms, past any detrimental detours, on through the wilderness of your life, and into the promised land. You can do it!

Mine is a journey of faith in each footstep of life I take. If I try to get too far ahead of myself, that is when I get stressed. So, I press onward each day, loving, serving, teaching, and relying on God for all things. With His help, I have climbed a few of the mountains of life both real and symbolic, step by step. I am going to keep on climbing until I reach my ultimate goal—returning to God with my family where I will be forever "normal for me"!

DIAGNOSIS SURVIVAL GUIDE

12 Tips to Survive and Thrive in Tough Times

by Tamara K. Anderson

RECEIVING A DIAGNOSIS IS AGONIZING. I know. I've been there—in a hospital waiting room, the minutes ticking by like a slow bass drum. You try to ignore the knots in your stomach while your head spins with endless thoughts and questions:

When will they be back? I wonder what the results of the testing will be? How long until I know the diagnosis? Will life ever be the same? I hope they are mistaken, and everything will be fine.

Diagnosis

Ordinarily, people feel one of two emotions (or perhaps a combination of the two) as they face a diagnosis: 1. Relief or 2. Devastation.

1. **Relief:** You feel relief at finally having a name

for what has changed your life. You feel validated knowing something was wrong. You feel a sense of purpose to learn what you can do to fight and even overcome this challenge.

For example, I felt tremendous relief when my oldest son finally received a diagnosis that his eyes were not tracking together. I had been to a multitude of doctors—even optometrists that couldn't find anything wrong with him. And yet he still struggled with reading (in 4th grade).

When I finally went to a developmental optician and they gave him a diagnosis, I almost cried with relief. Now that we had a proper diagnosis, the rigorous treatment and therapy could begin.

2. **Devastation:** You receive a diagnosis with utter devastation. Diagnosis hits some with the force of a tsunami wave. This tsunami changes, shifts, and alters your world: autism, cancer, paralysis, diabetes, or depression—any diagnosis has the strength to force a life detour or change of course.

When my second son was diagnosed with autism, I fell into the devastation camp. Whatever fleeting relief I felt was completely overpowered by the shock of the official diagnosis. I knew there was no cure for autism.

I barely contained my emotions through the end of the meeting, then I ran from the room and cried for the entire three-and-a-half-hour drive home. The diagnosis crushed my life's plan! I watched my dreams swirl down a dark drain, devouring every ounce of joy and happiness for the future.

What was I left with?

Fear.

- Fear of the monster diagnosis that had just swallowed my dreams.
- Fear of the future.
- Fear I knew *nothing* about this diagnosis.
- Fear I couldn't and didn't aspire to climb this dark, foreboding mountain placed in my path.

Since that day, my life has been one of extremes: crippling sorrow and magical joy. At times, those extreme emotions happen in one day or last for a season.

I have learned to ride this diagnosis roller coaster . . . throwing my hands up and laughing for the thrill of it at times, while closing my eyes with fear and dread when approaching new and frightening scenarios.

I am writing this guide because I would have loved having some help along my new path. Now that I've figured out some things that are useful and work, I'd like to share what I have learned with others, so that it is easier for you than it was for me.

You can pretend I am right there with you giving you a hug and handing you the "cheats" or "hacks" for surviving diagnosis fear and navigating forward.

Consider my checklist as a "how to guide" to navigating a "new normal" with cautious apprehension—no matter the diagnosis.

I wrote this so others would realize in the darkest moment of life that they are not alone! Someone else has looked at that dark mountain of diagnosis, feeling that dizzying range of emotions, and can help guide you safely to the top.

So, let's climb this mountain—together.

– 1 –

CLING TO NORMAL ROUTINES

If you're going through hell, keep going.

– Attributed to Winston Churchill

When hitting a life detour, it's best to hold tight to the mundane details of daily life. In times of chaos and loss, your soul craves normality.

Facing the first day post-diagnosis, I would have rather stayed in bed and pulled the covers over my head. Unfortunately—or perhaps fortunately—I had young children who needed me, so I had to get up. I did the normal everyday things to survive: Showering, preparing breakfast, lunch, and dinner, playing with the kids, driving children to school, cleaning the house, reading a book, and singing children's songs (if you have kids in the house, you'll understand).

These were routines I had done thousands of times before, but simply trudging through the daily routine breathed life back into my shattered heart. I had survived one day! That evolved into one week, and then one month post-diagnosis. Hope began to blossom in my soul—maybe I could do this after all.

Not very long ago I was visiting a friend who was going through chemotherapy. She explained to me that she was still working a couple of days a week so she could feel "normal." This is a perfect example of what I am talking about. Her life had been side-tracked when the diagnosis of cancer was pronounced—so she clung to the things in her life that felt familiar and reassuring.

There is a psychological benefit to doing normal things in completely abnormal times. It is like eating comfort food for the brain—and we all love our comfort food or our normal routines—especially amid chaos.

Once a diagnosis hits, immerse yourself in your daily routines. Not only is there comfort in these daily routines, but you may be surprised at how these mundane things—that may have felt boring or even stressful—when viewed from the other side of a diagnosis, may become moments of gratitude or blessings. Following routines might just help with survival during the first day, the first week, and even the first year.

- 2 -

FORGET THE FUTURE — FOCUS ON TODAY

Fear of the future is worse than one's present.

– Quintilian

DOES THINKING of the future cause extreme worry?

Is finding hope an unimaginable or incomprehensible goal? How do people fathom the future when daily survival is completely overwhelming?

They don't.

When dreams lay shattered, it is crucial to lay aside the future for a moment, while processing the present.

Push earlier goals and expectations out of your mind and *simply survive today.*

Survival in the here and now is more important than figuring out what the next year will encompass. With the diagnosis fresh in my mind, I couldn't imagine living with the same stress for a year or two or ten.

The thought made me want to cry, weep, and give up.

Instead, I coached myself to stay focused on the present. I learned *life unfolds one day at a time*. It is best to deal with it on a minute-by-minute, day-by-day basis. God gives us the grace to survive moment to moment.

One of my friends, Lynn Wilkinson, who was an occupational therapist for forty years, has a saying: "Don't worry about tomorrow; God is already there."

That is what I did. I left the future to God—trusting He would open the right doors at the right time. I had to believe that He would continue to lift and strengthen and help me through His grace in the future. It was imperative to have faith and hope while I kept fighting and praying.

And gradually, I began to set little goals as I could process them. The professionals I worked with had a mountain of goals, but my goals came more slowly. Maybe this was because I was so close to the situation, and I had to live it every day. It simply took me longer to become steadier on my feet.

Daily survival turned into years, and now over a decade of growing pains mingled with moments of pure joy.

In the wake of survival mode, I can now thrive one day at a time.

– 3 –

BE GENTLE WITH GRIEF

Weeping may endure for a night, but joy cometh in the morning.

– Psalms 30:5

ELIZABETH KÜBLER-ROSS CREATED THE "grief cycle" to describe the process experienced by the terminally ill. Anyone facing a major life detour or diagnosis can experience the grief cycle due to the loss of dreams, hopes, health, ambitions, or desires.

How I wish someone would have explained on diagnosis day that I would grieve for the "normal" life I would never have. Realizing I would experience the grief cycle would have helped me recognize the emotions I was feeling were normal.

It took several years to wade through this difficult and very personal *Grief Cycle*:

1. *Denial* there was anything wrong;
2. *Anger* at the diagnosing physician and God;
3. The *bargaining* stage where I pleaded with God for healing;
4. Experiencing the weight of *depression* associated with loss; and
5. Finally coming to the *peace* of acceptance.

DENIAL: Yeah, I lived here for a while. It took me many months to come to terms with the fact that the diagnosis was indeed correct. But while I processed this, I did *not* want to tell anyone or talk about it. It was too painful!

My expectations and dreams for life had just been shattered, and I needed to grieve for them in my own private way. You will too. Acknowledge this, and then move forward when you feel ready.

Be aware that this isn't a stage you can rush, and the time spent at this point in the cycle is uniquely individual. It takes as much time as it takes.

Denial is a phase. Don't get stuck in it. This isn't healthy for you or your family. Denying there is a problem won't make it go away and only creates more challenges if it is not dealt with.

For those with friends or family members going through this cycle—the best advice I can give here is to be patient and supportive of your loved ones living in denial. And prayers probably wouldn't hurt.

ANGER: I wish someone had explained the importance of being gentle with myself. As a believer, I couldn't understand why I was so angry with God. I wish I wouldn't have felt guilt on top of grief for the emotions raging within.

I dumped all of this raw emotion on God. Thank goodness He is big enough to take it, and good enough to let me vent.

I realize now that anger—at God, my husband, and others (for no "apparent" reason), was part of my grief cycle. I can now forgive myself for feeling anger because I realize it was a completely normal part of grief.

It is easy to try to blame everyone and everything for the diagnosis instead of realizing that playing the blame game doesn't change the past or the present.

Another word of caution: some people get stuck in this anger phase. It may feel easier to blame others for the problem, but that ultimately doesn't help you move forward.

Forgiving yourself and others is liberating. If you aren't there yet, pray for the strength to leave anger behind.

Often we aren't strong enough to do this on our own, but God is always big enough to strengthen us to do things we can't do on our own. My mantra can be found in Philippians 4:13, "I can do all things through Christ which strengtheneth me."

Let it go! Leave anger behind. Be free. Move forward.

BARGAINING: I begged and pleaded with God for healing. I promised to read the scriptures more faithfully, attend church with renewed vigor, be kinder, more patient, or even give my first-born child, or donate everything to charity—well, you catch the drift. But yes, I have promised grandiose things—often beyond my ability to maintain—and I'm sure everyone else has too, at times.

I had faith God could work miracles, but I felt angrier and more frustrated when the miracle I prayed for didn't happen. My prayers weren't answered the way I desired.

I had to learn the hard way that true faith is believing that even though God has the power to heal, perhaps he won't—and trusting that is for the best. I knew God could see the end from the beginning, and I had to hold fast and hope that He had my best interest at heart—maybe from an eternal perspective, because I sure couldn't see it right then.

It has been fifteen years since our initial diagnosis, and I can now see a few of the character-building reasons my family had to endure through several difficult diagnosis.

Dealing with children that have life-long diagnosis has helped me recognize what is truly important in life. I was often so busy caretaking that anything unimportant really did fall out of my life. I simply didn't have time to keep up on the most fashionable styles or worry about my child belonging to the most elite sports team when I could barely get my son to have a BM in the toilet at age eight.

I have become more loving, caring, more empathetic, more trusting in God. And now, I am writing about my experiences so that I can bring hope to others who are going through hard times.

I remember those years of anger and bargaining. I wondered, "why me?"

I have learned that the answer is "why not me?" We each have difficulties that tax us to our limits and beyond.

I needed to go through something really awful and hard for many years so that I could understand and empathize with others. I needed to learn that no matter how exhausted or angry I was that God would still be there. I needed to walk a steep and very rocky road so that I could someday reach the summit stronger and wiser and enjoy the mountain vista.

If I could go back to my younger "bargaining-self" I'd wrap her in my arms and cry with her. Then I would cheer her up and say, "This is awful and difficult, but you will discover how strong you can become through this."

It is all about becoming.

DEPRESSION: This is the second reason it is important to be patient and gentle with yourself. It is a bitter pill to swallow a life-changing diagnosis.

This is what doctors refer to as situational depression. It occurs usually within 90-days of a diagnosis due to traumatic changes in life.

There will be days you don't want to move. There will be moments you wish you could simply fast-forward because they are *too hard!* I felt that way for a long time. For me it felt like diagnosis was a heavy backpack I had to now carry *everyday*. It was challenging to do some of the normal things I used to do with ease because of this psychological weight on my shoulders.

The difference between situational depression and clinical depression is usually a chemical imbalance that manifests itself in not being able to "bounce-back." If depression interferes with your normal routine for more than six months, consider visiting a trained professional (a doctor or therapist) to talk about your symptoms.

Most cases of situational depression will disappear on their own as long as the person takes care of themselves. This will include exercising, eating and sleeping well, discussing their troubles with family or close friends or even joining a support group.

Eventually, as with any physical or psychological weight, you become stronger as you are able to process the diagnosis. But when I was weak, I leaned on God and on my family. They got me through.

The key here is to keep moving forward. Even if you take two steps forward and one step back on a daily basis, that slow progress amounts to consistent movement in the right direction. Keep taking those daily baby steps.

I love the tale of the *Tortoise and the Hare*. The hare begins the race running forward past the turtle, but it was the turtle that won the race—because he kept moving and didn't get distracted along the way. Just keep moving by trudging through the daily chores of life and you will make it.

PEACE: I vividly remember the day I felt a lasting peace again. It was glorious! It was as if the Winter of my life had finally started thawing into Spring.

God helped me finally reach this stage—and it was

years after the first diagnosis, and following a second life-changing diagnosis in our family.

I felt moments of peace along the journey, but that final "I am okay with this diagnosis peace" took longer to reach. I am glad God was in it for the long haul with stubborn old me! I couldn't have made it without Him.

The keys for me were time and my relationship with God. I told God about the good, the bad and the ugly moments of every day. I prayed and vented every frustration to God.

There were many years of prayer and scripture study—because I felt empty inside. I felt broken. Thank goodness God loves broken things and can eventually help us heal as we turn to Him.

Attending church, praying, and studying the scriptures yoked me to God in a way that I could feel moments of peace even though my life was anything but peaceful.

An eventual peace that I was okay with how my life turned out—even though I never would have chosen this path settled on me. I felt joy again. I did feel stronger and more confident in myself and in the unique path I was walking with God. I truly was happy in the midst of my chaos.

FINAL THOUGHTS ABOUT THE GRIEF CYCLE: Most people don't trudge through in a linear fashion—it's more like a roller coaster. These emotions ebb and flow—and even though you have "passed through" one stage doesn't mean you won't revisit it again. I ultimately came around to peace after I battled with God for a while. Time and God are efficient healers.

Learn from my story and be gentle with yourself when adjusting to a "new normal." Grief is such a difficult beast to tame. Take credit for daily trudging through the raging emotions. Be patient. Peace will come eventually—I promise.

– 4 –

DIAGNOSIS DOESN'T DEFINE THE PERSON

See people for who they are – not the labels affixed to them.

At first, the diagnosis seemed to be all I could think about.

In the previous section, I described it as a heavy backpack. But this backpack was also like a sodden blanket, weighing heavily on my mind and suffocating all other thoughts. The problem was, I couldn't see very clearly through that blanket.

I eventually began to peek out from under the diagnosis blanket, and what I saw changed my perspective. My son had not changed at all due to the diagnosis. In fact, he was oblivious to the fact that he now had a "label." He was still my sweet boy. Whether he had a diagnosis or not, I was still going to love him. He was my son.

I learned something important that day: *A diagnosis doesn't define a person.* My son, Nathan, was still the same sweet soul he had always been. The diagnosis didn't change who he was.

Realizing this was part of my "ah-ha moment" as I processed and progressed past the situational depression caused by diagnosis.

The diagnosis was simply a way for professionals to name and properly treat an issue my son was experiencing. Post-diagnosis, the floodgates opened and the amount of help which followed surprised me. I didn't want the diagnosis, but we needed the help.

So, lift that heavy blanket and remember a diagnosis doesn't define a person—no matter if it is you or someone you love. Everything special, wonderful, unique—every quirk and characteristic, everything that defines you—is still there. A diagnosis doesn't erase any of that.

Take heart that a diagnosis doesn't make you less. If anything, it makes you become more: stronger, braver, empathetic, kinder, and wise.

– 5 –

JOURNALING AND GRATITUDE

Happiness depends more on the inward disposition of mind than on outward circumstances.

– Benjamin Franklin

It is easy to fall into the trap of seeing the negative when life comes crashing down. But I quickly discovered a great life hack that helped me find joy: using a journal.

Journaling allowed me a space to be brutally honest, especially on the worst days. It also helped me seek for the little moments of joy and peace, while I sorted through the difficulties.

Here are some journal entries where I share some joys, and some heartaches:

September 26, 2006

We love our little dog. Jacob actually wanted to

walk him on our family walk last night. That is quite a step for him because he used to be really afraid of the dog. It was also quite a sight to behold because Jacob was all over the place and I had to constantly untangle both Jacob and the dog because they would get caught in the leash.

I put Noelle in pig tails for the first time yesterday and she looked so cute. Of course she pulled them out about five minutes later, but at least we tried. Right now she is singing "teach me to walk in the light" as she tries to put her clothes back on (which she just took off). She is so cute, and stubborn. She is two! Oh, now she is naked. Better go.

September 27, 2006

This morning on the way to school Jordan was asking me why he doesn't have a normal brother that he can play with and talk to. We have had this discussion before, but it seemed particularly hard to answer this morning. I asked him why he thought Heavenly Father had sent Nathan to our family. He said that he didn't know. He said he wanted a twin brother or an older brother. I told him that Uncle Daniel was like his brother, and that made him feel better. Then, he got sad and said, "Nathan and Jacob are never going to get married and I will always be a cousin, not an Uncle." I told him that someday Noelle will get married and he will be an Uncle.

My heart is heavy right now. I feel bad that I don't have a better answer for Jordan. I wish that he

> did have brothers who could play with him. Jacob does play with Jordan, but it isn't quite the same. I guess I feel inadequate answering him as to why when I don't know or understand the "whys" myself.

I can now go back and remember both the good and the hard because I wrote these little snippets in my journal. I am thankful I wrote because it shares a little of my journey.

Some people have a journal where they *only* write about little daily mercies they see or experience. Think what a powerful weapon this would be to read on days that are particularly devastating!

I have a friend who keeps notebooks everywhere—one in her car, her purse, her nightstand and she writes wherever she can. She is able to record ideas, journal about grief, or write about daily tiny blessings God has poured out since losing her husband. It has helped her process, vent, and remember the good and the bad.

Journaling has numerous benefits to offer beyond increasing your gratitude. There is a host of scientific and anecdotal support of this transformative tool. Among other things, journaling can:

- Provide clarity and insight into emotions and behavior
- Improve your success in changing habits
- Reduce stress
- Increase self-awareness
- Expand your perspective

- Act as a non-judgmental friend and counselor

Best of all, journaling is free, simple, and easy to do.

Grab a notebook and begin! Write about your joys, your sorrows, your shattered hopes, your dreams. Especially, write about the daily mercies or little miracles you see. Write a list of your blessings on particularly hard days: "I can breathe," "I can see," "I can love."

When life is the hardest, seek for and find daily miracles through journaling. Start your gratitude or mercies journal today!

– 6 –

PICK GOOD HEALTH CARE PROFESSIONALS

An apple a day keeps the doctor away.

– Benjamin Franklin

THERE IS NOTHING AS AWFUL as a bad health care provider—they are in and out, too busy to care. They are too overly confident that they have all the answers, and they don't listen to your thoughts and ideas.

Conversely, there is nothing as relieving as a fantastic doctor, nurse, or therapist—the ones that feel it is their life calling to help and serve. I have visited and dealt with multiple health care professionals through the years.

The health care professionals I enjoyed working with were the ones who:

- Willingly listened
- Were specialists in my area of need
- Communicated well—especially with the patient
- Were personable and caring—especially of those with a disability
- Gave honest feedback
- Admitted they didn't know everything
- Researched and presented the best options with competency
- Were flexible enough to include my thoughts/ feelings in the decision process
- Kept options open for treatment as different people react differently

Not sure where to begin your search? Ask around—nurses, other doctors, therapists, and especially in support groups. A question I found helpful: "If you were in my position, who would you pick as your doctor/ therapist?"

The answers to these questions helped me find efficient, knowledgeable professionals who collaborated during the diagnosis, through treatment, and into the prognosis process.

Sometimes finding the right professional for diagnosis can be tricky. I remember visiting several doctors when I was worried about one of my children. The answers they gave just didn't fit with what I was seeing.

I finally prayed and asked God to help me know

how to help my child. During the prayer, I suddenly remembered visiting a doctor's office about five years before for one of my other children. I found that doctor's information, called and set up an appointment, and finally got the right diagnosis and therapy for my child.

Go with your gut on choosing good health care providers. If you feel you need a second opinion, get it. If you feel you would work better with someone else, change. Find the right health professionals that fit with you, your beliefs, and your personality.

I am thankful I kept looking and found the right people to help me not only through one diagnosis, but a few others of different family members a few years later.

– 7 –

OVERCOME FEAR THROUGH LEARNING

Nothing in life is to be feared, it is only to be understood. Now is the time to understand more, so that we may fear less.

– Marie Curie

It is always frightening to face the unknown. Sometimes it would seem easier to stick our head in a hole like an ostrich and hope it will go away, but unfortunately, this doesn't work with a diagnosis. It can be painful to push through the fear and begin the quest to learn about the diagnosis.

Keep this in mind: Knowledge helps overcome fear.

Researching online made me feel like a little boat in a giant storm—tossed this way and that with so many thoughts and opinions. I didn't know which person to believe.

Knowledge empowers you when it comes from proven sources. Ask a doctor or other professional for reliable sources of information on the diagnosis.

The first person you need to listen to and learn from is the diagnosing physician and any technicians or therapists you are working with. This is their area of expertise.

If you are forgetful or feel overloaded with information when you are listening to a professional, ask if you can record their advice so that you can go back and listen and "digest" their counsel. It also helps to have a friend or family member go with you to any appointments so they can help you remember what the doctor says. You can also ask for copies of printed or electronic documents they can share with you about your diagnosis.

I love asking questions. One of my college professors once said, "Does anyone have a question besides Tamara?" Write your questions down before appointments so that you can maximize your time with your doctor and learn the answers to the questions you have about your particular diagnosis.

As you increase your understanding about the diagnosis, it leads to educated decisions and improved problem solving in coordination with professionals. You are a team working to move forward, and you'll find your fear diminishing.

– 8 –

BUILD A SUPPORT NETWORK

Grief knits two hearts in closer bonds than happiness ever can; and common sufferings are far stronger links than common joys.

– Alphonse de Lamartine

When facing any diagnosis, a valuable tool is an effective support network. It is too difficult to be strong all the time by yourself. Having a support network will give you trusted people to talk to and with whom you can share pain, sorrow, and grief.

Support Network Suggestions:

- Spouse
- Extended family
- Friends
- Teachers
- Therapists

- Online or local support groups
- Doctors
- Church organizations/pastors/God
- Respite providers (check online for ones in your area)

One of the hardest things about building a support network is learning to ask for help. Talking to friends naturally flowed into "How are you doing?" Instead of saying "fine," I had to learn to say, "You know, I am really struggling right now."

Often, I just needed a listening ear. For some reason, talking through my problems with a sympathetic soul helped me feel better and find ideas or answers I might not have considered before.

If you feel like you need to talk and no one is around, you can talk out loud to yourself or vent to God. Remember that you are processing information and life-changing events, so it is okay to vocally try to figure out solutions to your diagnosis dilemma.

Most people want to help, but they just don't always know what to do. If you struggle asking for help, remember that when you let others help and serve you and your family, you are blessing them by giving them an opportunity to serve. And as they serve you, you learn to love them more and they learn to love you more. Service = love.

Sometimes friends would ask, "Is there anything I can do to help?" I couldn't always think of something in the moment, but reassured them that if I thought of something, I would let them know.

Then I had to swallow my pride and let them know if I thought of an area where I did need help. This conversation could look like this: "I need help brainstorming a solution to a problem. Would you mind helping me think of solutions?"

Tap the fantastic resources in your network. I remember asking questions to a teacher who was an expert with many years of experience in our diagnosis. I even shadowed her for a day so I could glean a bit of what she knew and watch her in action.

I am also part of a local support group and a private online support group on Facebook. It is an amazing resource for people to ask questions, share tips, and even grieve together. I have felt my heart break at some of the discussions we have, but we keep it real and it is nice to be in a place where people love you and don't judge because they have, "been there and done that."

Seek out and build this network. You'll gain relief along with the added strength that comes from sharing a heavy burden. I would never have survived if not for the help of my earthly angels. They stood by me as I cried, brainstormed, laughed, strategized, worked, and ate chocolate.

– 9 –

STAY INVOLVED THROUGH SERVICE

What is the essence of life?
To serve others and to do good.

– Aristotle

One of the best lessons I learned was how essential it was to continue to serve, stay involved, and help others. My burdens felt lighter as I helped and served others, and my despair lifted over time. It feels good to be needed.

Service is something that fits into and fills the cracks of our busy lives.

Serving looks differently for each person. The key is to look beyond yourself. Ask, *What are my passions? What skills do I have? Could I be a listening ear for someone else walking down diagnosis road?* That is a good place to begin.

If you are dealing with health challenges, remember to pace yourself. You do need to take care of yourself and perhaps be creative in the way you serve. Maybe you can text or call friends or family when you have little to no energy. Getting out of the house is also a big psychological boost.

Service ideas:

- Write an encouraging note to a friend
- Participate in online support groups or charity events
- Reach out to others going through the same diagnosis
- Put together kits for those pushing through chemo (or any other diagnosis you are passionate about)
- Collect items for shelters or charities (first aid supplies, socks, hygiene supplies)
- Volunteer for church group
- Share a smile with a stranger
- Produce/donate needed items (quilts, blankets, hats, scarfs)
- Volunteer at schools/hospitals
- Index genealogy records online
- Donate cans to a food pantry

Side note for caregivers: Be sure that you have things that you are involved in outside of caring for your loved one. This is critical to your mental health and allows you a break from the stresses of everyday life. Maybe it is service, maybe it is work, or maybe it is developing a talent. Don't feel guilty for spending some quality "you time" to rejuvenate. You need it and you will be a better caregiver as you take care of yourself.

One of my favorite online videos is a terminally ill, ninety-one-year-old man sitting in a hospital bed, using a hat loom to knit hats for the homeless. He explained it gave him purpose. It also brought him joy to help others. Joseph Addison explained it best when he said, "No one is more cherished in this world than someone who lightens the burden of another."

– 10 –

PLAN FOR STRESS RELIEF

With the fearful strain that is on me night and day, if I did not laugh I should die.

– Abraham Lincoln

ANY DIAGNOSIS CAN CAUSE an increase in stress—whether you are the patient or the caregiver. During this time, stress relief is crucial. There have been days when my anxiety peaked, and I knew I needed a release.

Here is a list of tips which have helped myself and others through the years:

- Meditating
- Deep breathing
- Receiving a massage
- Doing yoga
- Listening to or playing music
- Laughing

- Exercising
- Reading a good book
- Watching happy movies
- Napping
- Journaling
- Taking a walk, hike, or drive
- Getting respite help—if you are a caregiver, make sure you get a break!

Which stress relievers appeal to you?

My favorite stress relievers are walking, singing inspiring music, napping, or reading a fun book.

For example, when stress seems to have my insides churning, I feel the need to walk—and even sporadically run it off. Taking my frustrations out in a positive way, with my feet hitting the pavement, helps calm that churning into a more manageable emotion. It also gives me the natural "high" of the endorphins created by exercising.

Singing at the top of my lungs when I am stressed also helps relieve stress. Not only am I breathing deeply to sing, but singing positive and uplifting songs motivate me.

Books have always been an escape for me. I prefer fantasy, adventure, and a twist of romance because real life stories are sometimes too real for me. I live with raw stress and emotions daily. When I read, I want to find myself in a different place, far away from my own challenges for a moment.

Special note: I don't encourage using drugs, alcohol, binge eating, or scrolling mindlessly through social media as stress relievers. These activities are addicting and will not help you progress through grief. They will only give an addiction on top of a diagnosis. Be wise.

I find it helpful to make a list of healthy stress relieving activities and how long it will take to do them. This is an example of a list I keep on my phone of stress relievers I can do when I take a quick break.

If I have 5 minutes I can:

- walk up and down the stairs a couple of times
- go outside to breathe some fresh air
- listen to my favorite song and sing along
- pray
- read my favorite comic strip

If I have 10 minutes I know I can:

- do a short exercise routine
- read a distracting book (although I have to set a timer when I read)
- journal
- play a game

If I have 20 minutes I can:

- nap
- clean an area of my home (while dancing to music)
- take my dog for a walk
- call a friend to catch up and laugh

Can you see how purposeful planning helps you maximize your relaxation time?

If you are a caregiver—please remember to take care of yourself so that you can continue to take care of others.

No matter what, make a list of stress relievers and pick a few favorites to sprinkle throughout your day. Be sure to tuck a few ideas inside your "Emotional Survival Kit" for particularly challenging days. When emotions run high, practice those favorite stress relief options. They'll help you survive another day with your sanity intact.

– 11 –

THE BIGGEST TRAP—COMPARISON

Comparison is the thief of joy.

– Theodore Roosevelt

Some of my heaviest moments came when I compared myself to others. This is one of the easiest and biggest traps that people fall into.

One particularly difficult evening when I was despairing over how much our diagnosis impacted our quality of life, I poured my soul out to God asking why I couldn't have a "normal" family that could do normal things.

The answer whispered in my heart, "Tamara, this is normal for you."

It was a tremendous "ah-ha" moment for me. My life was totally normal for me. Even though it was easy to compare myself to other people and families, I realized that God didn't want me to compare. I was normal for me. Our family was normal for us.

You and I are going to progress through diagnosis in completely unique and different ways because our bodies are different, and our perspectives and experiences are distinctive from anyone else's. We are each incredible, wonderful, and original.

One of the things I notice about comparison is that I always seem to compare my weaknesses to others' strengths. That is like putting an Olympic basketball star next to a gymnast and comparing the two at basketball. They are built differently, they have each worked at developing differing skills and abilities, so the gymnast is never going to be the basketball star.

For some reason this comparison seems so easy to understand, but so hard to apply. Whatever you do, remember when you watch people that you are seeing their best, so don't compare it to your worst.

Don't get discouraged when perhaps the typical treatment may not work for you as it worked for cousin George. We are each different. Keep moving forward and work with your team of health providers to find what does help and work for you or your loved one.

This is *your* journey, not anyone else's. Don't compare. Everyone is different and will go through life's struggles at a different pace—and this is perfectly okay. You are normal for you.

– 12 –

RESISTANCE TRAINING & JOY

Always remember, you have within you the strength, the patience, and the passion to reach for the stars to change the world.

– Harriet Tubman

My major in college was Therapeutic Recreation. In my course of study I learned about and studied the muscles in the human body. The process by which muscles grow and become stronger was fascinating to me.

If we don't use our muscles, they deteriorate or atrophy. Think about a person who becomes paralyzed. Their muscles shrink because they are not using them.

I learned that if there was no resistance or opposition to the muscle, there was no strength. There must be resistance training for muscles to grow stronger.

The same thing can be said of each of us in life—if we do not use or build our life muscles during times of resistance or trial, we do not grow stronger.

As much as I hated each diagnosis and it's ensuing stress upon me and my family, I gradually learned that God was helping me build some life muscles. Now, I know I complained and put up quite a fit. I didn't want to build muscles right then. I wanted to coast along and enjoy life.

But life ebbs and flows. There are times that are strenuous and we are pushing with all our might—like a cyclist pedaling up a giant hill. And there will be times when we get to coast a little down the other side—until we hit the next hill.

The ultimate goal, of course, is to be strong with God and to find joy in the journey.

The principle behind Therapeutic Recreation is to find an activity that the person enjoys so much they won't think about the exercise or pain involved.

For example, we would instigate some competitive games of Balloon Volleyball. Stroke victims were suddenly trying to use both arms because they wanted to get that balloon to the other side of the court. They were building muscles and they didn't even realize it.

I think we can apply this same principle in life. Try to have a little bit of fun daily. You can also search for and find the smallest joyful moments that happen daily: breathing, smelling, eating, laughing, seeing sunny skies after long, dark nights, smiling, or calling/texting loved ones.

One of the elderly ladies at the Rehab Center where I worked was so very happy. I loved working with her and being around her. She was a shining ray of joy.

One particular Veteran's Day, this cheerful woman

stood and wept openly as she told us of her husband, whom she married before he left to serve in World War II. Unfortunately, he never returned home from the war, but gave his life in defense of freedom. She never remarried.

This amazingly cheerful woman had figured out a way to build some life muscles during hard times and to come through with joy after experiencing sorrow. She is a shining example that was burned into my memory of someone who could find peace and happiness despite enduring difficult challenges.

She had built strong life muscles amid hardship and come through with joy. I knew I wanted to be just like her "when I grew up" but I would never have picked the sorrow that it took to get there.

When resistance comes into our lives we have a choice, we can face it "happily or unhappily" (as I tell my children). Sometimes we do a little bit of both. Don't let your trials make you bitter. Let your trials make you stronger and choose joy!

CONCLUSION

My goal is to spread hope during hard times. Diagnosis is one of those times when life can get hard. I hope that by sharing these tips with you, you have felt uplifted, been inspired, and are motivated to keep going.

As you move forward, remember these tips:

1. Cling To Normal Routines
2. Forget the Future—Focus on Today
3. Be Gentle With Grief
4. Diagnosis Doesn't Define the Person
5. Journaling and Gratitude
6. Pick Good Health Care Professionals
7. Overcome Fear Through Learning
8. Build a Support Network
9. Stay Involved Through Service
10. Plan for Stress Relief
11. The Biggest Trap—Comparison
12. Resistance Training & Joy

You will have hard days and you will have good days along your diagnosis journey. But no matter what you do, keep moving forward. Don't you give up. Never give up!

I know you probably would not have chosen this path. I wouldn't have either. But the experience and knowledge we gain trudging this path less traveled helps us become stronger, more capable, more compassionate, more loving, more kind, more thoughtful, more grateful, more wise, more real. You are *more* because you are on this journey.

The price for wisdom is experience—and you are having lots of experiences right now.

I invite you to share your nuggets of wisdom with those you encounter along the diagnosis road. Become a beacon of hope to those who are struggling. Love freely. Journey with joy.

When you feel weak, pray for strength. The truth is we are never strong enough to make this journey alone. The challenges we face in life will always be too hard, but they are never too hard for God. So, yoke yourself to Him and He will help you carry your heavy burden.

"When you're in a dark place, you sometimes tend to think you've been buried.

Perhaps you've been planted.

Bloom!"

I *love* this quote! I have felt buried at many points in my life, and just like the bulbs that have to exert all their effort to push their green chutes heavenward at the Spring thaw, I too have had to push heavenward in those dark times.

What happens next is the miracle of turning to God in hard times—you do indeed bloom in spite of and perhaps because of the most difficult challenges in life. Bloom my friends! Bloom!

No matter what, keep trudging up your mountain. Ride your diagnosis roller-coaster with faith and knowledge, not fear and despair. You can do this! I believe in you!

CALL TO ACTION

If you have been inspired by this book, please tell others about it. Together we can help each other survive any life detours and diagnosis because we know we aren't alone.

I love to hear from my readers. You can contact me on my website: tamarakanderson.com.

ACKNOWLEDGMENTS

Special thanks to God for helping me through midnight until dawn and giving me these little tidbits of understanding and enlightenment throughout life—which I now share with you.

A big thank you goes to Jenny Wright for giving me the idea to write this book in the first place. Thanks also to my husband, Justin Anderson, my parents Jim and Karen Klein, my sister Lisa Layton, and Lisa Johnson for their help as I began my writing journey.

I owe a tremendous amount of gratitude to my mentor, Richard Paul Evans. He picked me up when I was a little boat in a big ocean and taught me how to navigate this crazy world of writing and publishing. Then he gave me a group of boats to sail with—and special thanks go out to my Premier Author Training groups. Thanks for being my "go to" people when I needed a second opinion. I love all of you! I also love Rick's staff: Diane, Jenna, Heather, and Laurie Liss—the world's best agent that I never got to use (because I self-published)! Someday, Ms. Liss, someday ☺.

Thanks also to another mentor of mine, Benjamin Hardy, who gave me the final push to just get this book published! I am so grateful to Ben and his AMP group for helping me overcome my fear by focusing more on my vision or my "why" and letting that motivate me.

I also must thank Dayna, Jenni, Andrew, Myra, Heidi, Maddy, Fran, Lisa, Tim, and Jerald—thank you for your wisdom, edits, expert marketing advice, and getting me from A-Z. Thanks to my walking buddies Molly, Jeanette, Vickie, and Nicholle who encouraged me as I updated them on my writing and all my crazy plans. A special shout-out to Mardee who lets me just show up at her home and listens to me, the excerpts of my book, and keeps me sane. And to all my other friends and family members who have helped me along this detoured path for many years, *thank you* for loving me and my family.

And what would I have ever learned if I didn't have four kids to chase around?! I love you Jordan, Nathan, Jacob and Noelle and am so thankful to be your mother.

And finally, thank you dear reader, for giving the gift of your time to read my book. I love connecting with my readers and hearing your stories!

Do you have a story to share about what God has taught you? Do you know someone I should interview on my podcast, *Stories of Hope in Hard Times*? Please feel free contact me at:

tamarakanderson.com • instagram.com/tamarakanderson

facebook.com/tamarakanderson • Twitter: @tamarakanderson

ABOUT THE AUTHOR

TAMARA LOVES READING STORIES with happy endings, conducting choirs, and juggling the activities of her four children. She is the mother of three boys (two of which are on the autism spectrum) and one girl. Raising her brood is a full-time job! Tamara loves learning—both in and out of the classroom, but prefers reading books for fun. She has lived in the east, south, and west of the United States and even in Argentina for three years as a young girl. Tamara enjoys podcasting, gardening, writing, singing, chocolate, and going on dates with her husband, Justin.

Made in the USA
Columbia, SC
03 April 2019